ELEVATE

For Gopal and Darley,
my unbeatable parents.
You've given me opportunity,
you've given me everything.

and for Anna,
my best friend and my wife.
We make a bloody great team.

ELEVATE

EVERYDAY INGREDIENTS, INCREDIBLE FLAVOURS

BRIN PIRATHAPAN

PAVILION

CONTENTS

INTRODUCTION 7

FEELING FRESH 15

PICKY BITS 45

HEARTY COMFORT 73

TWIST 109

GF GLUTEN FREE
EF EGG-FREE
V VEGETARIAN
Ve VEGAN
P PESCATARIAN

GREAT COMPANY	**143**
SWEET TREATS	**179**
TIPS & TRICKS	**199**

INDEX	216
ACKNOWLEDGEMENTS	222
ABOUT THE AUTHOR	223

INTRODUCTION

Cooking, for me, has always been an act of elevating the most basic ingredients into plates full of vibrancy. Growing up, our table was full of flavour and colour, and I guess my palate was accustomed to eating well. We were graced with Tamil Sri Lankan food every night: bright yellow dhals (or parippu as we call it), deep brown mutton or chicken curries, bold purple beetroots and refreshing green spinach. Dinner was a colour palette that transferred effortlessly to flavour. Even the nights that saw my parents branching out to European dishes like Spaghetti Bolognese or a simple jacket potato, there'd still be a strong undertone of Jaffna curry powder and a spicy tingle... meat and two veg just didn't exist in our household.

It's not until recently that I've been able to look back and truly appreciate the food I grew up on. Nourishing and vegetable-heavy, I do now kick the younger me for the nights I asked for frozen pizza instead of the beautiful food my parents had made. Although my cooking style isn't entirely Tamil based, it takes huge inspiration from the culture and the food I grew up eating. It's not easy to create a table full of bold flavours that comes together in harmony, but that's exactly what my parents, uncles and aunties did. I truly think that is where my love of boldness and vibrancy, and my ability to balance them, comes from.

Of course, there are smatterings of my Tamil Sri Lankan background that empower some of my dishes, but there are just as many influences from many other parts of the world. From Sichuan province, whose food can numb and tingle your mouth in such an addictive way, to lesser-known Italian dishes that bring warmth and comfort with every mouthful – you'll find that, in this book, I don't stick to the rules and boundaries of cultural cuisine. I'm not trying to create fusion food per se, but I'm doing my best to show how blurred the boundaries between cultures and cuisines are. More importantly, I want to show how intensely delicious food can be when we allow ourselves to combine the flavour-based lessons that our cultures have learnt over centuries. The reason for such diversity in my food is because my culinary creativity is a total amalgamation of my Tamil background and my British upbringing; rich with food from all over the world, thanks to the diverse nature of this country and the opportunities my parents have given me. Travel naturally plays into my love for global flavours and I owe a lot of that to my lovely wife, Anna. Anna's always instilled in me the importance of travel and enjoyment instead of fixating on work or other trivial worries. It's the reason we've seen the world together, which has had a big impact on the way I cook. Frankly, it's also a huge factor in why I'm here writing this book as part of this whole new world I've had the pleasure of delving in to.

Once I started cooking as a university student, I quickly discovered a need for budgeting but was unwilling to compromise on flavour. They say beggars can't be choosers, but I wanted to make incredible food on a student budget – and it wasn't impossible. I would often scout out the best deals and reduced-price ingredients (regardless of my familiarity with them) and head home to research what tasty dish I could create with my haul. There was a lot of trial and error, learning what worked together and what didn't; testing out flavours that I'd heard of but hadn't yet tried. I still remember the first day I cooked celeriac and thinking to myself 'Damn, this tastes like celery… and I really hate celery'. But it was an important lesson that helped me learn how to remove the attributes I didn't like by using new techniques. I found that I could enhance the caramel-like sweetness that comes from celeriac when it was roasted, which removed it's celery-like bitter crunch. Over a decade on from starting university, I'm still constantly learning, using trial and error, to create recipes. What I have learnt so far has built the collection of recipes in this book: some that have come from familiar flavour combinations and others that are a result of the boundaries I pushed while I trialled (and errored) – but they're all certainly delicious.

Creativity is important to me. I didn't know that until I started in this wonderful world, after five years working as a vet. For my whole life, I've been on a fairly rigid path: studying hard for a 'respectable' degree and securing a 'prestigious' job. But, since leaving school, I had no opportunity to take advantage of the creative urge that I've always had in me. I went from being a school student, engrossed in art and music, to a university

student who craved a creative outlet that fitted around my career path. We've all got to eat several times a day, so food felt like a natural starting point!

My cookery journey reached new heights when I was accepted to join the 20th series of *MasterChef*. I've always watched *MasterChef* at home with my family. Even once I'd fled the nest, I'd still call my dad to make sure he knew when the new series was starting. I'd reached a point with my cooking where I finally felt ready to put myself in a difficult position – as well as a point in my career where I was ready to try something new. I knew that if I didn't apply that year I'd be sitting at home watching the show, wishing it was me cooking (and probably thinking I could do better... how arrogant!).

The first round was called 'Basic to Brilliant' and, looking back now, I realize that I was truly in my element. I chose onions as my basic ingredient and showed off their versatility by cooking and presenting them in six different ways – miso onions, spring onion purée, crispy shallots, pickled shallot shells, shallot granola and a spring onion garnish. It didn't occur to me until later in the series that I'd been practising this concept of elevation ever since I started cooking. Since winning the series and giving up my day job to become fully thrusted into the world of food, I knew my first book had to be based on this concept: basic ingredients made beautiful and brilliant.

Cooking has always felt like a hobby, a release and a type of therapy to me – I guess a career change into the culinary world was my version of running away with my therapist. I believe even the most stressful day can be escaped by locking yourself away in the kitchen for an hour or two to produce (and eat) something comforting, nourishing and homely. Even after making the big move from veterinary medicine to food, I still find time in the kitchen invaluable. It's a place to create and be free – a time to forget about the trials and tribulations of a whole new career! I'm not saying everyone needs a drastic career change to eat and cook well – or even to scratch the creative itch that many of us have. Frankly, there's no need for you to do that because that is exactly what this book is made for. The recipes are your catalyst for transforming bad days into good ones and relieving any stress. I want you to feel a sense of pride when you eat the food you make from these recipes. They may be my dishes, but they can still be your creative outlet.

I've spoken at length about the positive impact food has had on my life, the almost medicinal effect it's had on my happiness. I won't for one second pretend this will be the case for everyone, but I do truly believe it'll be the case for many. If you've had a challenging day, week or month, I want you to be able to pick up this book and flick to a recipe that feels exciting. I want to you to be able to immerse yourself in it to clear your head from the negativity: to come out with an end product, a plate of food, that makes you breathe a sigh of relief. A realization that the last 20 minutes, hour, or even 3 hours have flown by without remembering the initial stress that prompted you to pick up the book and start cooking. I hope this book gives you the tools to embed a little bit of culinary creative release into your daily routine.

THIS BOOK HAS THREE AIMS:

The first and most obvious is the elevation of basic ingredients into delicious plates of food. Cans of tuna become moreish, spicy bites of pure joy (see page 56), frozen parathas transform into a delicious dessert (see page 190) and humble aubergines rise into juicy and flavoursome showstoppers (see page 104).

The second is to elevate your skills as a home cook; with small tips and tricks (see pages 199–215) that make everyday cooking easier, more enjoyable and more efficient. Small things, like learning how to julienne carrots or even a mango, will provide you with more confidence in the kitchen and provide you with the tools to tackle cooking from scratch at more mealtimes.

The third and final is maybe the most important to me: the elevation of mood and how food can totally alter your day in the greatest way. Whether it's as simple as a warming bowl on a rainy day, a fresh plate of greens after a weekend of overindulgence, or a sweet treat because you deserve it after the day you've had – there's a subsection of food that aligns

INGREDIENTS ▲

SKILLS ▲

MOOD ▲

itself to every mood. That's how this book and its chapters work – from Feeling Fresh (see pages 15–43), to Great Company (see pages 143–77), to Picky Bits (see pages 45–71) or Sweet Treats (see pages 179–97), you can find the right food for your mood.

Although I've been creating recipes and content for a while now, seeing this book in my hands feels a lot like my first piece of art, something to frame, something to be proud of. It represents a lot. On the surface, it represents who I am and how I like to eat and cook – but, on a deeper level, it represents freedom, change and, dare I say, bravery. It was easy to leave my old world and try and make something of this new one, but it was harder to persevere and get through the lulls. I've loved writing this book – the early starts when the creative parts of my brain are harnessed best, and the late nights eating all the tested food with friends around the table (because frankly, there's no way two people can, or should, consume that much food in one night!).

I want you to delve into this book in whatever way suits you. If you find you've got an odd ingredient at home that needs using up, flick to the index (see page 216) and find the recipe that elevates that one ingredient into a bold and beautiful dish.

Maybe you're not sure what you'd like to eat? Work out what mood you're in and head to a chapter that satisfies it – whether you're in need of some Hearty Comfort (see pages 73–107) or you're feeling adventurous with a hankering for a Twist (see pages 109–41).

If you feel like levelling up your skills, find a tip or trick from the section at the back (see pages 199–215) and pick a recipe that utilizes it. The next time you need to fillet a chicken thigh or butterfly a round fish like mackerel, you'll do it easily and be filled with pride.

Make this book work for you. There's no one way to use it.
- Brin

FEELING
FRESH

CABBAGE

GF, EF, V

Most of my dinners at home include a slaw or pickle of sorts and it's a great way to add crunch and acidity – two really important tricks to use when you're trying to elevate a meal. I feel like white cabbage has been branded as pretty bland and boring but a simple recipe like this brings life back into it with fresh and vibrant notes. You can find fresh curry leaves from a local South Asian supermarket, where they're very cheap for a big bunch. You can even freeze them and use them straight from the freezer in future. Frying them here imparts an earthy, slightly citrus aroma that pairs wonderfully with cabbage to make it a little bit more complex and interesting.

CURRY LEAF SLAW

SERVES: 6   **TIME: 15 MINUTES**   **DIFFICULTY: 1/3**

4 tbsp olive oil
20 fresh curry leaves
½ sweetheart cabbage, cut into thin strips
1 Granny Smith apple, cored (no need to peel) and cut into matchsticks
50 ml/2 fl oz apple cider vinegar
finely grated zest and juice of 1 lime
1 tbsp honey
salt

Add 2 tablespoons of the olive oil to a small frying pan over a medium heat.

Add the curry leaves and cook until they start to crackle a bit and release their smell, about 2 minutes. Remove from the heat and place the curry leaves on kitchen paper to soak up any excess oil.

Add the cabbage, apple and curry leaves to a serving bowl.

In a clean small jam jar with a lid, combine the remaining 2 tablespoons of olive oil, the apple cider vinegar, lime zest and juice and honey. Shake well to mix, then pour over the slaw. Add a sprinkle of salt and mix well.

Allow to sit at room temperature for at least 30 minutes (or refrigerate if making ahead of time) before tucking in, and give it a couple of mixes during this time.

GF, EF, V

I struggle with bitter flavours, it's the reason I don't like grapefruit and why I don't like negronis even after years of forcing myself to drink them because, let's admit it, they are undoubtedly cool. However, I still enjoy cooking with bitter ingredients, like chicory, because it's a great way to understand how certain flavours, such as saltiness and sweetness, can balance out others like bitterness. That balancing act means this salad is nowhere near as bitter as a negroni but is most certainly just as cool, or maybe even cooler.

CHARRED CHICORY & PEACHES

SERVES: 4 **TIME: 20 MINUTES** **DIFFICULTY: 1/3**

- **2 chicory,** each cut into quarters lengthways
- **olive oil,** for drizzling
- **4 ripe peaches,** stoned and each cut into 8 wedges
- **50 g/2 oz (shelled) pistachios**
- **2 sprigs of fresh tarragon**
- **1 ball of mozzarella or burrata,** drained

For the dressing
- 1 tbsp olive oil
- 2 tbsp honey
- 2 tbsp balsamic vinegar

Place the chicory quarters in a bowl. Drizzle some olive oil over them, then mix and toss so each piece is coated a little.

Place a frying pan over a high heat and, once hot, place the chicory quarters, cut side down, in the pan. Once you get a bit of char, flip to the other cut side. Remove the charred chicory and place back in the bowl.

Place the peach wedges in the same hot frying pan with a little olive oil until they also char and caramelize slightly on the cut sides, turning once. Then add them to the chicory in the bowl.

Turn the heat down to medium and add the pistachios. Keep them moving so they don't burn but toast them slightly, about 3 minutes. Tip them on to a chopping board and roughly cut them so they're about half the original size.

To make the dressing, combine all the ingredients in a small bowl and whisk together. Alternatively, you can combine them in a jar and shake well. Pour this over the charred chicory and peaches. Sprinkle the toasted pistachios on top, then strip the leaves from the tarragon sprigs and add these to the bowl too.

Give everything a toss to coat in the dressing, then arrange it on a serving plate or platter. Tear the mozzarella or burrata into pieces and place it haphazardly over the salad, then serve.

MACKEREL

GF, EF, P

Romesco is a Catalonian sauce supposedly created by fishermen to accompany the fish they caught, which explains why it goes so well with this simple butterflied mackerel. It's also a sauce that can be altered to your liking, so versions of this vary from family to family, in Catalonia anyway. I've swapped out classic blanched almonds for hazelnuts, which adds a whole new level of complexity to this sauce. Check out my tips on how to butterfly mackerel on page 210 and pair this dish with crispy, smoky Batata Harra (see page 57) for a fresh summer dinner.

BUTTERFLIED MACKEREL WITH HAZELNUT ROMESCO

SERVES: 2 **TIME: 1 HOUR** **DIFFICULTY: 2/3**

2 red peppers
½ red onion
1 red chilli (if you like it hot)
50 g/1¾ oz cherry tomatoes
2 garlic cloves, peeled but left whole
2 tbsp olive oil, plus extra for drizzling and brushing

50 g/1¾ oz blanched hazelnuts
1 tbsp red wine vinegar
juice of 1 lemon
2 whole mackerel, butterflied (see page 210)
sea salt and freshly cracked black pepper

For the pickled red onions
1 red onion, thinly sliced
2 tbsp apple cider vinegar
juice of 1 lime
2 tbsp olive oil
pinch of sea salt

Start by making the romesco sauce. Preheat the oven to 180°C fan/200°C/400°F/gas mark 6.

Add the whole red peppers, red onion, red chilli (if using), the cherry tomatoes and the garlic cloves to a roasting tray, drizzle with olive oil and sprinkle with salt.

Roast in the oven for 30 minutes, then add the hazelnuts and return to the oven for another 10 minutes.

While the peppers are roasting, make the pickled red onions. Place the red onion slices in a bowl with the apple cider vinegar, lime juice, olive oil and salt. Mix well and massage with your fingers, then set aside.

Once the peppers have roasted, cool slightly, then carefully (as they will be hot!) remove the stems and seeds but try to hold on to the lovely juices inside the peppers.

Add all the roasted ingredients to a blender along with the 2 tablespoons of olive oil, the red wine vinegar and lemon juice. Blend to a paste, but it's ok if it's a bit lumpy. Set aside.

Preheat the grill to high. Season the butterflied mackerel with salt and black pepper all over and brush with olive oil.

Place the mackerel on an oven tray (preferably on a rack) under the grill, skin side down, and cook for 2 minutes, then flip and cook, skin side up, for 5 minutes or until the skin is crispy.

Spread the vibrant romesco sauce on a serving plate or platter and lay the grilled butterflied mackerel fillets on top. Top with the pickled red onions and a side of Batata Harra (see page 57).

EF, V, Ve

Roasting kale can be a bit of a challenge. You can go from lovely vibrant green, soft leaves to black, bitter crunch in the space of a couple of minutes. This recipe takes all of that risk away and 'cooks' the kale without cooking it at all. With a bit of tender love and care (and salt), you can massage the kale to relieve the bitter flavours and make it vibrant, soft and delicious.

BRASSIC FATTOUSH

SERVES: 6   **TIME:** 30 MINUTES   **DIFFICULTY:** 1/3

4 pitta breads
olive oil, for drizzling
2 tsp sea salt, plus extra for seasoning
280 g/10 oz kale
15 g/½ oz fresh parsley
15 g/½ oz fresh mint leaves
300 g/10½ oz baby plum tomatoes, quartered
1 green pepper, deseeded and finely diced
½ cucumber, finely diced
4 radishes, thinly sliced
4 spring onions, thinly sliced
150 g/5½ oz pomegranate seeds

For the dressing
2 tbsp olive oil
1 tbsp apple cider vinegar
1 tbsp pomegranate molasses or balsamic vinegar
juice of 1 lemon
2 garlic cloves, grated
1 tsp sumac
1 tsp dried mint
good pinch *each* of sea salt and freshly cracked black pepper

Preheat the oven to 180°C fan/200°C/400°F/gas mark 6.

Cut the pitta breads into bite-sized pieces and add them to a large baking tray with a hefty drizzle of olive oil and a sprinkle of salt. Bake in the oven for about 20 minutes, turning halfway. They should become dark brown with a decent crunch. Remove and set aside to cool.

Meanwhile, remove all the tough stems from the kale and add it to a bowl with the measured salt. Rub the kale and salt together with your hands for about 5 minutes. Really massage the kale and press it in the palm of your hands. As it starts to soften and become a brighter green, tear the kale with every rub to make a shredded texture.

Chiffonade the parsley and the mint leaves (see page 204).

Add the tomatoes, green pepper, cucumber, radishes, spring onions and herbs to a serving bowl along with the pomegranate seeds and the massaged kale. Toss together to mix.

To make the dressing, add all the ingredients to a clean jam jar with a lid. Give it a good shake to create a lovely dressing. Drizzle this over the salad and mix thoroughly so the dressing gets into every crevice.

Add the baked pitta pieces just before serving and mix well.

GF, EF, P

This dish is traditionally made with puntarelle – a Catalonian chicory with long thin stems. Unfortunately, puntarelle is not readily available in the UK, but my version uses chicory and choy sum to create a lovely twist on this Italian classic. The choy sum and chicory come together to add both the texture and bitterness so familiar in a classic Puntarelle alla Romana. Everything is wrapped in a delicious anchovy-heavy dressing that mellows out the bitterness from the chicory and balances this dish perfectly.

CHICORY & CHOY SUM ALLA ROMANA

SERVES: 4   **TIME: 10 MINUTES**   **DIFFICULTY: 1/3**

- 2 chicory
- 2 choy sum
- 100 ml/3½ fl oz olive oil
- 1 tbsp red wine vinegar
- 6 canned anchovy fillets
- 2 garlic cloves, peeled but left whole
- 1 red chilli
- good pinch of flaky sea salt

Cut the root off the chicory, then remove the leaves one by one. Stack them up and slice them lengthways into 2-cm/¾-inch-thick strands. Place the cut pieces in a bowl of ice-cold water.

Cut the root off the choy sum, then cut the long stems in half. Place the choy sum in a heatproof bowl, cover with boiling water and leave for 2 minutes, then remove and place in the bowl of ice-cold water until ready to use.

Add all the remaining ingredients to a blender and blend together to create a creamy dressing.

Remove the leaves from the ice bath (squeeze out any excess water) and place in a serving bowl. Pour over the dressing and toss well so each leaf is coated, then serve.

NEW POTATOES

GF, EF, P

Potato salads are great but I always feel like they need more and when you give them more you allow them to be paired with food that's much more interesting. The tahini in this recipe comes together with the harissa salmon to create a dish that's refreshing and summery but also interesting and intriguing. Serve alongside a few green leaves like rocket or a leafy salad for an extra bit of freshness.

TAHINI YOGURT POTATO SALAD & HARISSA SALMON

SERVES: 4   **TIME: 30 MINUTES**   **DIFFICULTY: 1/3**

750 g/1 lb 10 oz new potatoes, any large ones cut in half
3 tbsp harissa paste
2 tbsp honey
4 salmon fillets
olive oil, for drizzling
1 red onion, finely diced
20 g/¾ oz fresh coriander leaves, finely chopped
10 g/¼ oz fresh mint leaves, finely chopped
a few fresh chives, finely chopped
100 g/3½ oz pomegranate seeds
sea salt

For the yogurt dressing
3 tbsp natural yogurt
1 tbsp tahini
juice of ½ lemon
2 tsp sumac
sea salt and freshly cracked black pepper

Add the potatoes to a large saucepan with cold, heavily salted water – always start potatoes in cold water to get an even cook. Bring to the boil over a medium-high heat and cook until fork-tender. Drain and steam-dry for about 5 minutes, then set aside to cool.

Combine the harissa paste and honey in a mixing bowl, then add the salmon fillets. Mix to coat all over and leave to marinate for about 10 minutes.

Meanwhile, preheat the oven to 180°C fan/200°C/400°F/gas mark 6. Line a baking tray with greaseproof paper.

Place the marinated salmon on the lined baking tray, drizzle over some olive oil, then bake in the oven for 12–15 minutes until cooked through and opaque.

For the yogurt dressing, add all the ingredients to a mixing bowl, season with salt and a decent crack of black pepper and whisk together. Add the red onion and herbs to the dressing, along with the cooked potatoes. Add three-quarters of the pomegranate seeds and bring everything together.

Sprinkle the remainder of the pomegranate seeds on top of the potato salad and serve alongside the cooked salmon fillets.

GF, EF, V

Lockdown for me, as for many people, centred around food and experimenting with new dishes. I was living with my now wife and two friends of ours. One of these friends was Nic, a half-German, half-Guatemalan fella with a wealth of global culinary experiences behind him and an appetite to match. Nic introduced me to the beauty of maleta, proper refried black beans that reached the perfect consistency when the beans formed one homogeneous fluid texture that flopped into this smooth structure when flipped in a pan. I love making this dish – a big plate of those beans topped with chirmol (a Guatemalan charred tomato salsa) and feta – and scooping it all onto slightly toasted tortillas. It's a fantastic dish to serve as part of a spread and a great way to use up those cans of black beans you've had in the cupboard for the last few months...

MALETA DE FRIJOLES CON CHIRMOL

SERVES: 4–6 **TIME: 45 MINUTES** **DIFFICULTY: 2/3**

3 x 400 g/14 oz cans black beans
5 tbsp olive oil
1 white onion, roughly chopped
3 garlic cloves, roughly chopped
2 tsp ground cumin
2 tsp paprika
200 g/7 oz feta cheese
sea salt
coriander, to garnish

For the chirmol
3 ripe tomatoes
1 white onion, finely diced
15 g/½ oz fresh coriander, chopped
1 red chilli, finely chopped
glug of olive oil
juice of 1 lime
pinch of sea salt

Preheat the oven to 180°C fan/200°C/400°F/gas mark 6.

Drain one can of black beans, thoroughly wash the beans, then drain again and dry on a tea towel.

Add these dried beans to a large baking tray, add 1 tablespoon of the olive oil and season with salt. Mix well, then cook in the oven for 30 minutes, mixing them halfway through, until crispy. This can also be done in an air fryer at 200°C/400°F for 10–15 minutes. Set aside.

CONTINUED OVERLEAF

Meanwhile, make the chirmol. Place the whole tomatoes in a frying pan over a high heat without any oil and let them char a bit on all sides, about 10 minutes. If you have a blowtorch, you can do this with that instead.

Once charred, roughly dice the tomatoes, then add to a bowl with all the remaining chirmol ingredients and mix well. Set aside.

Add 2 tablespoons of the olive oil to a large frying pan or sauté pan over a medium-high heat. Once the oil is hot, add the chopped onion and garlic.

Once the onion starts to colour a bit, add the cumin and paprika. Mix everything together well and cook for a couple of minutes, then add the remaining two cans of black beans including their juices. Cook over a medium-high heat with a lid on for 10 minutes.

Add everything from the pan to a food processor, along with 200 ml/ 7 fl oz of water and blend to a paste.

Add the remaining 2 tablespoons of olive oil to the pan you previously used and heat over a medium-high heat. Add the black bean paste back in and keep stirring for about 5 minutes. It's ready when it darkens a bit and forms a spreadable consistency, similar to hummus.

To serve, spread it out on a plate, then top with the chirmol and crispy black beans. Finally, crumble the feta all over. You can serve with flatbreads to scoop this up, place it in a taco or eat it alongside grilled meat.

GF (USE GF SOURDOUGH), EF, V

Courgettes always seem to be the bridesmaid and never the bride, but this recipe finally gives them the chance to be the main event. The slight char adds depth and excitement to the courgettes, similar to the transformation meat can undergo when it hits a barbecue. This salad is bursting full of fresh ingredients that bring different flavour notes to make the humble courgette really sing.

COURGETTE CRUNCH

SERVES: 4 **TIME: 35 MINUTES** **DIFFICULTY: 1/3**

- 200 g/7 oz sourdough (preferably stale), cut into cubes
- 2 tbsp olive oil, plus extra for drizzling
- 3 courgettes
- 360 g/12½ oz asparagus spears, trimmed (hard bottoms cut off) and cut into 4–5 cm/ 1½–2 inch pieces
- finely grated zest of 1 lemon
- 200 g/7 oz feta cheese
- 20 g/¾ oz fresh mint leaves
- 50 g/1¾ oz (shelled) pistachios
- salt

For the hot dressing
- juice of 1 lemon
- 2 tbsp honey
- 1 tbsp apple cider vinegar
- 1 tbsp olive oil
- ½ tsp chilli flakes

Preheat the oven to 180°C fan/200°C/400°F/gas mark 6.

Place the bread cubes in a roasting tin. Drizzle with a healthy glug of olive oil, toss to coat and then roast in the oven until crispy, about 20 minutes, turning halfway through. Set aside.

Meanwhile, cut the courgettes using the cut-and-roll technique (see page 200).

Add 1 tablespoon of the olive oil to a large frying pan and place over a medium-high heat. Place the courgettes, flesh side down, in the pan and cook until slightly coloured/charred, then flip to the other side. Season both sides of the courgettes as they cook. Once both sides are coloured, about 8 minutes altogether, add to a large mixing bowl. You may have to do this in two batches.

Add the remaining 1 tablespoon of olive oil to the same frying pan along with the asparagus and cook over a high heat until slightly charred and a more vibrant green colour. This will take 4–5 minutes. Add these to the mixing bowl as well.

Add the lemon zest to the bowl, then crumble in the feta as well.

Chiffonade the mint leaves (see page 204) and add to the bowl.

Add the pistachios to a small dry frying pan and toast them over a medium heat for 3 minutes, moving them around every minute. When they're done, roughly chop them into small pieces (about half their original size).

Make the hot dressing. Add all the dressing ingredients to a small saucepan over a medium heat and allow the mixture to boil for a minute, then take it off the heat.

Add the sourdough croûtons to the veg bowl along with the toasted pistachios. Cover everything in the hot dressing, then mix it all together and serve.

GF, EF

Finding ways to eat food that tastes like the meals you eat for comfort but feels like the meals you eat for health is the biggest hack for eating well. This salad tastes like the best lamb doner you've ever had, but leaves you feeling energized and nourished instead of stodgy and regretful. You could even put this salad straight into a wrap for a real kebab experience with none of the guilt.

SPICED LAMB & ROASTED CHICKPEA SALAD

SERVES: 4 **TIME: 40 MINUTES** **DIFFICULTY: 2/3**

400 g/14 oz can chickpeas, drained and rinsed
2 tsp paprika
3 tbsp olive oil, plus an extra splash
500 g/1 lb 2 oz minced lamb
3 tsp sumac
1 tsp dried mint
1 tsp ground cumin
1 tsp ground coriander
½ tsp ground cinnamon
1 red onion, finely sliced
juice of 2 lemons
about 200 g/7 oz kale, tough stems discarded and leaves sliced
½ cucumber, diced
1 ripe avocado, peeled, stoned and diced
150 g/5½ oz baby plum tomatoes, cut into quarters
handful of fresh mint leaves, finely chopped
handful of fresh parsley, finely chopped
handful of pomegranate seeds
sea salt

Preheat the oven to 180°C fan/200°C/400°F/gas mark 6. Add the chickpeas to a bowl with 1 teaspoon of the paprika, a sprinkle of salt and 1 tablespoon of the olive oil. Mix well, then spread out on a baking tray and roast in the oven for 25 minutes until slightly crispy. Remove and set aside.

Meanwhile, add the minced lamb to a frying pan over a medium-high heat with a splash of olive oil and cook, stirring occasionally to break it up. When it starts to brown, add the remaining paprika, 1 teaspoon of the sumac, the dried mint, cumin, coriander, cinnamon and a sprinkle of salt. Mix well. Cook until you start to get crispy bits of lamb, about 12 minutes, then remove from the heat and set aside.

In the meantime, add the red onion to a bowl with the lemon juice, the remaining sumac, the remaining olive oil and a pinch of salt and mix well. Set aside.

Add the kale to a separate bowl. Sprinkle with salt and massage with your hands for 5 minutes to soften.

Add the cucumber, avocado and tomatoes to the kale, along with the herbs, and toss gently to mix.

Add most of the spiced lamb to the salad, along with most of the crispy chickpeas, most of the sumac onions (with the juices from the onions) and a sprinkle of the pomegranate seeds. Mix everything together, then plate up. Top with the remaining spiced lamb, crispy chickpeas, sumac onions and pomegranate seeds and tuck in.

RHUBARB

GF, EF, V

I'm a massive fan of rhubarb in savoury dishes. It has the ability to cover both the sweet and acidic portions of the flavour profile, which I find to be two important elements involved in the elevation of any dish. This delicious spring salad is fresh but earthy with the goat's cheese and has plenty of texture from the al dente courgettes and toasted nuts.

ROASTED RHUBARB & GOAT'S CHEESE SALAD

SERVES: 2 **TIME: 35 MINUTES** **DIFFICULTY: 1/3**

3 sticks of rhubarb, cut into 2.5 cm/ 1 inch pieces
½ tbsp caster sugar
2 courgettes, cut into rough chunks
splash of olive oil
180 g/6¼ oz asparagus spears, trimmed (hard ends cut off) and cut into 2.5 cm/1 inch pieces
10 fresh mint leaves
handful of (shelled) pistachios, roughly chopped
2 tbsp pine nuts
4 tbsp balsamic vinegar
2 tbsp honey
juice of 1 lemon
30 g/1 oz rocket
100 g/3½ oz soft goat's cheese
sea salt

Preheat the oven to 180°C fan/200°C/400°F/gas mark 6.

Spread the rhubarb pieces on a baking tray, add the sugar and a sprinkle of salt and toss to mix. Roast in the oven for 15 minutes until it's a vibrant pink and slightly softened.

Meanwhile, char the courgette chunks with a splash of olive oil in a pan over a medium-high heat until coloured on two sides. This should be enough to cook them but have a tiny bit of a bite left. The char adds a nice bit of smoke to the dish too.

Remove the courgettes to a plate, then add the asparagus pieces to the pan with 1 tablespoon of water. Cover with a lid and leave to steam for a few minutes until just tender.

In the meantime, chiffonade the mint (see page 204).

Add the pistachios and pine nuts to a small dry pan and cook over a medium heat until slightly toasted, about 3 minutes (see Cook's Tip).

Add the balsamic vinegar, honey and lemon juice to a separate small saucepan and heat over a medium heat while mixing until slightly thick and sticky (watch carefully as it can easily burn). Remove from the heat.

Add the courgettes, asparagus, rhubarb, rocket, mint and most of the mixed nuts to a bowl and mix well. Plate up and scatter the goat's cheese all over. Drizzle with the hot glaze and top with the remaining nuts, then serve.

COOK'S TIP → You can also toast nuts and seeds in the microwave – place them on a plate and heat on high for 30 seconds, move them around and then repeat until you get a nice toasted colour on them.

EF, P

Fish and fruit can be quite a scary combination, but my favourite mouthful of this recipe is one with tuna and a segment of orange. The orange adds a sweet acidity that massively elevates the tuna's delicate, buttery flavour without overpowering it. When you combine this with the slight aniseed notes of the fennel, you get a salad that has flavour dancing all around it. A perfect dinner for a summery evening.

SESAME TUNA WITH FENNEL AND ORANGE

SERVES: 2   **TIME: 20 MINUTES**   **DIFFICULTY: 2/3**

1 fennel bulb
1 orange
small bunch of fresh dill, roughly chopped, plus extra to garnish
small bunch of fresh coriander, roughly chopped, plus extra to garnish
40 g/1½ oz rocket
1 tbsp honey
1 tbsp light soy sauce
1 tuna steak
100 g/3½ oz mixed black and white sesame seeds (or just use white seeds if that's what you have)
2 tbsp olive oil

For the dressing
zest and juice of ½ orange
1 tbsp olive oil
1 tbsp light soy sauce
½ tbsp apple cider vinegar
1 garlic clove, grated
½ tsp chilli flakes

Thinly slice the fennel on a mandoline, or with a knife, and add to a large mixing bowl along with dill, coriander and rocket. Set aside.

Peel the orange, removing as much pith as possible (this is often done more effectively with a knife instead of a peeler). Cut out the segments of orange by running a knife along the white lines. Set these aside.

Combine the honey and soy sauce in a bowl and mix well. Coat the tuna in this mixture.

Add the sesame seeds to a tray, then add the tuna, getting a good crust all over. Pat the seeds down but don't rub them.

Heat the olive oil in a frying pan over a medium-high heat. Once it's hot, add the tuna and cook on each side for about 30–60 seconds. Remove from the heat.

For the dressing, add all the ingredients to a small bowl and mix together (see Cook's Tip). Set aside.

Add the dressing to the fennel mixture and mix well, then spread on a platter. Slice the tuna and arrange the slices over the salad. Finish with the segments of orange and some extra dill and coriander leaves.

COOK'S TIP → I always keep empty jam jars (with lids) to make salad dressings. Simply add the ingredients to the clean jar, place the lid on tightly, then give everything a good shake – it works like a charm.

GF, EF, V, Ve

Sugar snap peas seem to get overlooked these days, but their freshness and crunch mean they can bring a lot to the table. Adding a slight char to them builds another layer of flavour that makes this unassuming vegetable more complex and intriguing. This simple recipe coats the peas in a sharp and spicy dressing and is bound to become a go-to for any summer meal or barbecue.

SPICY SUGAR SNAP PEA SALAD

SERVES: 4 **TIME: 25 MINUTES** **DIFFICULTY: 1/3**

1 tbsp olive oil
2 garlic cloves, thinly sliced
1–2 tsp chilli flakes (or 1–2 tsp crispy chilli oil)
360 g/12½ oz sugar snap peas
small handful of salted peanuts, roughly chopped
small handful of crispy onions (see Cook's Tip for homemade, GF option)

For the pickled red onions
½ red onion, thinly sliced
2 tbsp apple cider vinegar
2 tbsp olive oil
finely grated zest and juice of 1 lime
pinch of flaky sea salt

Make the pickled red onions. Add the red onion to a small bowl along with the apple cider vinegar, olive oil, lime zest and juice and the flaky salt. Mix really well (massaging slightly can speed up the pickling process too), then set aside.

Prepare the sugar snap pea salad. In a cold large frying pan or wok, add the olive oil, garlic slices and chilli flakes (or crispy chilli oil) and place over a medium heat.

Once the garlic slices start to colour, add the sugar snap peas and turn the heat up to high. Toss the contents of the pan occasionally and cook until the peas become vibrant green with some charring, about 3 minutes.

Drain the liquid from the pickled red onions and add it to the pan with the peas. Turn the heat down to low, then let this bubble away for a couple of minutes and mix it all together, before transferring the peas (along with the juices in the pan) to a serving bowl. Add the pickled red onions and toss to mix.

Add the peanuts to the frying pan or wok that the peas were cooked in. Place over a medium heat and cook until the peanuts start to get some colour, about 2 minutes. Add them to the sugar snap peas. Toss everything together, then sprinkle with the crispy onions and serve.

COOK'S TIP → You can either buy ready-made crispy onions or make them yourself. To make them yourself, follow these few simple steps:

Cut an onion in half and slice into thin strips. Break up the slices so all the strands are separate.

Add the onion slices to a small saucepan and cover with sunflower or vegetable oil.

Cook over a medium heat, stirring occasionally. Once the onion slices start to brown and become crispy, remove them from the oil with a slotted spoon and drain on kitchen paper to soak up any excess oil. You'll need to act fast once they start to brown as they can easily overcook and burn.

P

I try to get as many brassicas into my diet as I can – I love their taste and they make me feel good. Wrapping them in a home-made Caesar salad dressing only enhances them further. My one non-negotiable for this dish is home-made croûtons – so simple to make but so unbelievably delicious. Train your mind to make croûtons whenever you've got stale bread in the house and I guarantee you'll increase salad consumption 10-fold.

CAVOLO NERO CAESAR SALAD

SERVES: 4 **TIME: 35 MINUTES** **DIFFICULTY: 1/3**

150 g/5½ oz sourdough (ideally stale but doesn't matter too much!)
olive oil, for drizzling
2 tsp chilli flakes
400 g/14 oz cavolo nero
flaky sea salt

For the dressing
6 canned anchovy fillets
1 tbsp capers, drained
juice of 1 lemon
1 tsp Dijon mustard
1 tbsp mayonnaise
2 tbsp olive oil
2 garlic cloves, peeled but left whole
40 g/1½ oz Parmesan cheese, finely grated, plus extra for garnish
1 tsp sea salt
good crack of black pepper

Preheat the oven to 180°C fan/200°C/400°F/gas mark 6.

Slice the bread thickly, then cut into cubes. Add to a large baking tray and drizzle generously with olive oil. Sprinkle with flaky salt and the chilli flakes, then give it all a good mix.

Bake in the oven for 20 minutes, turning halfway through, until golden and crisp.

Meanwhile, strip the cavolo nero leaves from their stems and place in a large heatproof bowl. Pour boiling water over the cavolo nero and leave submerged for 2 minutes, then tip the leaves into a colander or sieve, drain off the water and set aside to drip.

Add all the dressing ingredients to a blender and blend together until smooth. Set aside.

Once the croûtons are done, remove them from the baking tray and transfer to a large salad bowl. Set aside.

Place the cavolo nero in the same baking tray that the croûtons came out of, place back in the oven and cook for 5–10 minutes, turning halfway through.

Add the cavolo nero to the croûtons and drizzle on the dressing. Mix it all together and serve up with extra Parmesan shavings.

GF, EF, V

I used to hate the flavour of aniseed and it's without doubt solely down to the horrible amount of sambuca shots I unwillingly (arguably willingly) consumed at university. I've since tackled my fear and opened my eyes to using it in cooking and it now features quite regularly in my recipes. As with a lot of strong, sometimes polarizing flavours, it's just about learning how to use them to create a flavour you like. When combining aniseed (in the form of star anise) with sweet carrots it becomes warming and fragrant instead of harsh and in-your-face. It's also a fantastic way to make the humble carrot a showstopping and exciting party piece.

ANISE CARROTS & WHIPPED RICOTTA

SERVES: 6   **TIME: 30 MINUTES**   **DIFFICULTY: 1/3**

1 kg/2 lb 4 oz carrots
3 tbsp olive oil
4 star anise
50 g/1¾ oz salted butter
1 tbsp light brown sugar
200 ml/7 fl oz vegetable stock
500 g/1 lb 2 oz ricotta
finely grated zest of 1 lemon
1 tsp flaky sea salt
freshly cracked black pepper

Peel the carrots and cut them into irregular wedges using the cut-and-roll technique (see page 200). Try to make the carrots similar in size so they cook evenly.

Add 1 tablespoon of the olive oil to a frying pan over a medium-high heat. Add the carrots and star anise and cook until the carrots get a bit of colour on two sides, about 8 minutes.

Turn down the heat, add the butter and sugar and cook gently until the butter and sugar have melted.

Add the vegetable stock and simmer with a lid on for about 10 minutes, then another 10 minutes with the lid off until the liquid reduces and the carrots are just fork-tender.

In the meantime, add the ricotta to a bowl with the lemon zest, the remaining 2 tablespoons of olive oil, the salt and a good crack of black pepper. Whisk well, ideally with an electric whisk to make the ricotta smooth and light.

Spread the whipped ricotta on a serving plate and pile the carrots on top. Drizzle the remaining juices from the pan all over the carrots and serve.

PICKY
BITS

EF *plus salting

I'd love to give you a profound memory or event that inspired me to create this recipe, but frankly, I just wanted to create a dish based around the phrase 'knuckle sarnie'. There's no pun more sophisticated than responding 'I'll give you a knuckle sarnie' when a mate barges into your house and demands food – which you can imagine happens to me a lot. But I'll tell you what, I'd risk a knuckle sarnie any day if this was what I was getting. Pair with the Curry Leaf Slaw on page 16.

KNUCKLE SARNIE WITH SPICED APPLE JAM

SERVES: 4 **TIME: 3¾ HOURS*** **DIFFICULTY: 3/3**

- 3 pork knuckles/hocks
- 1 tbsp fennel seeds
- 1 tbsp coriander seeds
- 1 tsp Sichuan peppercorns
- 1 brown onion, roughly chopped
- 1 carrot, roughly chopped
- 4 garlic cloves, roughly chopped
- 2.5 cm/1 inch piece of fresh ginger, peeled and roughly chopped
- 500 ml/18 fl oz dry cider
- 400 ml/14 fl oz chicken stock
- 100 ml/3½ fl oz boiling water
- 2 tbsp Spiced Apple Jam (see overleaf)
- sea salt

Pat the skin of the pork knuckles/hocks dry, then heavily salt the skin and set aside for 1 hour. If you can do this step 24 hours ahead of time and refrigerate the salty pork for 24 hours, your chances of a crispy skin will be much higher.

Preheat the oven to 140°C fan/160°C/300°F/gas mark 3.

Make the spice rub by combining and crushing the fennel seeds, coriander seeds and Sichuan peppercorns in a pestle and mortar or spice grinder until you get a coarse powder.

Throw the onion, carrot, garlic and ginger into a roasting tray that can also take a wire rack placed on top. Add the cider and chicken stock to the roasting tray as well. Place a wire rack over the top.

Pat the salted pork dry, then dust off any excess salt.

Season the pork all over with the spice rub mixture, then place the upright on the wire rack over the veg and liquid. Roast in the oven for 2½ hours.

Increase the oven temperature to 220°C fan/240°C/475°F/gas mark 9 (or the highest your oven will go). Remove the pork from the oven and strain the juices from the roasting tray into a saucepan (discard what is left in the sieve). Return the pork to the hot oven and roast for a further 30 minutes until the skin is crispy. Alternatively, you can skip this step and pull the skin off and stick it in an air fryer at 200°C/400°F for 10 minutes instead.

CONTINUED OVERLEAF

To serve
8 slices of bread of your choice
Spiced Apple Jam (see recipe below)
Curry Leaf Slaw (see page 16)

Remove the pork from the oven and leave to rest, uncovered, while you make the sauce. Add the boiling water to the roasting tray and mix it around, collecting all the lovely flavours from the bottom of the tray. Strain into the saucepan with the other juices and add the spiced apple jam. Simmer until you're left with a thick, sticky sauce that can coat the back of a spoon.

Use two forks to pull the meat off the pork and shred it (discard the bones), then add this to the sauce you've just made.

Toast your bread, then spread a layer of spiced apple jam on one side of four slices. Top with the pulled pork mixture and some Curry Leaf Slaw. Finish off the sarnies with the other slices of bread on top and tuck in!

SPICED APPLE JAM

MAKES: 250–300 ML/9–10 FL OZ

4 Granny Smith apples, peeled, cored and diced
125 g/4½ oz caster sugar
80 ml/2½ fl oz apple cider vinegar
1 tsp ground fennel
1 tsp ground Sichuan peppercorns
½ tsp ground cinnamon
1 star anise

Add all the ingredients to a saucepan, along with 150 ml/5 fl oz of water.

Bring to a simmer, then cook for about 15 minutes, until the apples are soft, stirring occasionally.

Remove the pan from the heat and discard the star anise, then mash the mixture with the back of a fork. Use as required. The jam will last in a clean, airtight container in the refrigerator for about two weeks. Perfect with cheese or with your Sunday pork roast.

V

I love cauliflower but my love is not unconditional. It cannot be soggy, it must have a slight char to it and it should ideally be lathered in some kind of delicious sauce. There are two recipes that do this perfectly, cauliflower cheese and this Korean-Style Bang Bang Cauliflower. This recipe takes soggy and sometimes bland cauliflower and makes it crispy, fiery and moreish – replace your crisps and dips with some of these bad boys at your next dinner party to get people going from the moment they walk in.

KOREAN-STYLE BANG BANG CAULIFLOWER

SERVES: 6 **TIME: 1 HOUR 5 MINUTES** **DIFFICULTY: 1/3**

60 g/2 oz plain flour
1 tsp gochugaru or chilli flakes
1 tsp onion powder
1 tsp garlic powder
½ tsp sea salt
125 ml/4 fl oz milk
2 eggs
1 large cauliflower, broken into florets
100 g/3½ oz panko breadcrumbs

For the sauce
125 ml/4 fl oz light soy sauce
2 tbsp gochujang
3 tbsp honey
1 tbsp sesame oil
1 tbsp rice wine vinegar
juice of 1 lime

To garnish
1 tbsp sesame seeds
1 spring onion, finely sliced
1 red chilli, finely sliced

Preheat the oven to 180°C fan/200°C/400°F/gas mark 6.

Combine the flour, gochugaru or chilli flakes, onion powder, garlic powder and salt in a mixing bowl.

In a separate bowl, whisk together the milk and eggs. Slowly add the wet mix to the dry mix, while whisking, to produce a runny batter.

Dunk the cauli florets into the batter to coat. Allow the excess batter to drip off back into the bowl, then add the florets to a bowl of the panko breadcrumbs, one by one, and coat fully. Transfer to a wire rack placed over a baking tray.

Roast in the oven for 20 minutes, then turn each floret and go in for another 20 minutes until crispy on the outside but soft on the inside. Alternatively, you can roast these in an air fryer at 200°C/400°F for 12–14 minutes, turning once.

Meanwhile, make the sauce. Add all the ingredients to a small saucepan and mix well. Heat over a low-medium heat until thick and glossy, stirring regularly.

Remove the roasted cauli florets from the oven, they should be golden brown with a few speckles of char. Coat in the sauce. Mix gently but well so that every nook and cranny is coated in the sauce!

Garnish with the sesame seeds, spring onion and chilli and enjoy!

*plus marinating time

As you can imagine, this was very much a festive creation for me. We all love cranberry sauce with roast turkey, so it seemed like a natural progression to experiment with chicken wings. The sweetness of cranberry sauce and the savoury spice of gochujang complement each other perfectly and result in a sticky, delicious mess all over your fingers and mouth. Perfect.

KOREAN CRANBERRY CHICKEN WINGS

MAKES: ABOUT 20–28 WINGS   **TIME: 45 MINUTES***   **DIFFICULTY: 2/3**

1 kg/2 lb 4 oz chicken wings
vegetable or sunflower oil, for deep-frying
mixed black and white sesame seeds, to garnish

For the buttermilk marinade
500 ml/18 fl oz buttermilk
1 egg
1 tsp gochugaru or other chilli flakes
1 tsp onion powder
1 tsp garlic powder
½ tsp sea salt

For the coating
250 g/9 oz cornflour
1 tsp gochugaru or other chilli flakes
1 tsp onion powder
1 tsp garlic powder
1 tsp sea salt

For the sauce
4 tbsp light soy sauce
3 tbsp cranberry sauce
2 tbsp gochujang
2 tbsp rice wine vinegar
1 tsp sesame oil

For the kewpie dressing
2 tbsp kewpie mayonnaise
juice of ½ lime
1 tbsp sesame oil

Cut off the chicken wing tips and cut each wing into two pieces by slicing at the joint.

Add all the buttermilk marinade ingredients to a large bowl and mix well. Add the chicken, coat with the marinade, then cover and marinate for at least a couple of hours, ideally in the refrigerator overnight.

Meanwhile, in a separate large bowl or container (that has a lid), combine all the coating ingredients, mixing well.

Remove the wings from the marinade and allow them to drip off any excess, then drop into the coating mixture. Put the lid on the container and shake well to coat the wings. Discard the marinade.

Heat enough vegetable or sunflower oil in a deep-fat fryer or a heavy-based saucepan (don't fill the pan more than two-thirds full) to 180°C/350°F (or until a small piece of bread browns in 30 seconds). Deep-fry the wings (in batches) for about 12 minutes, turning halfway through, until deep golden brown and cooked through. Alternatively, cook them in an air fryer at 200°C/400°F for 25 minutes.

Meanwhile, to make the sauce, combine all the ingredients in a small pan and heat until it just boils, then turn off the heat. For the kewpie dressing, combine all the ingredients in a small bowl.

Coat the fried chicken wings in the sauce. Sprinkle with mixed sesame seeds and a drizzle of the kewpie dressing to serve and get stuck in.

Whenever I want to cook duck breasts, I always buy a whole duck and butcher it myself because it's so much cheaper. This means I've always got a steady stream of duck legs in the freezer that often end up being made into this deliciously moist recipe with crispy skin. Salt and pepper seasoning is so addictive, I could have it on most things and, since creating this recipe, I've always got a little pot on the go.

AIR-FRYER SALT & PEPPER DUCK PANCAKES

SERVES: 4   **TIME: 1 HOUR**   **DIFFICULTY: 1/3**

4 duck legs, skin-on
5 spring onions
½ cucumber
12 Chinese pancakes
hoisin sauce, to serve

For the salt and pepper seasoning
1 tsp sea salt
½ tsp Sichuan peppercorns
½ tsp chilli flakes
2 tsp caster sugar
½ tsp garlic powder
½ tsp ground ginger
¼ tsp ground cinnamon
½ tsp MSG (monosodium glutamate) (optional)

Start by making the salt and pepper seasoning. I like to use a spice grinder (or clean coffee grinder) but this can be done in a pestle and mortar too. Combine all the seasoning ingredients and grind/blend or pound to a coarse powder.

Pat the duck legs dry with kitchen paper, then use a fork to prick holes in the skin. There's no need to oil them as the fat in the skin will render out to help cook them.

Sprinkle the seasoning all over the legs (top and bottom) and then place them on an air fryer rack.

Preheat the air fryer to 140°C/300°F, then add the duck legs on the rack to the air fryer and cook for 40 minutes, skin-side up. After 40 minutes, increase the temperature to 210°C/410°F and cook for a further 5 minutes to crisp up the skin.

Meanwhile, julienne the spring onions and cucumber (see page 202) and steam the Chinese pancakes as instructed on the packet.

Once the duck legs are cooked, shred the meat and skin with two forks (discard the bones) and then assemble your pancakes, topping them with the duck, spring onions and cucumber. Serve with hoisin sauce on the side.

GF, EF   *plus resting

I love using sausage meat in a whole range of recipes – it provides a bit more flavour and structure to whatever you're creating. The heavy fennel notes in these bites goes perfectly with the pork, and the slightly fiery but sweet chutney packs a moreish punch. A great snack for any spread or a crowd-pleasing start to a dinner party.

SAUSAGE PAKORAS WITH A MANGO & CORIANDER CHUTNEY

MAKES: 20–24   **TIME: 45 MINUTES***   **DIFFICULTY: 2/3**

For the sausage pakora mixture
- 8 sausages of your choice (about 450–500 g/1 lb–1 lb 2 oz)
- 1 red onion, diced
- 1 carrot, diced
- 2 garlic cloves, grated
- 2.5 cm/1 inch piece of fresh ginger, peeled and grated
- 3 tbsp gram flour
- 1 tbsp cornflour
- 2 tsp sea salt
- 1 tsp fennel seeds
- 2 tsp ground cumin
- 2 tsp ground coriander
- 1 tsp chilli flakes
- ½ tsp ground fenugreek
- vegetable or sunflower oil, for deep-frying

For the mango and coriander chutney
- 1 ripe mango, peeled, stoned and roughly chopped
- 2 tbsp Greek-style yogurt
- finely grated zest and juice of 1 lime
- 1 green chilli
- 30 g/1 oz fresh coriander leaves
- 1 tsp sea salt

Make the pakora mixture. Slice open the sausage skins and scrape out the meat into a mixing bowl. Add all the remaining pakora ingredients, except the oil for frying, then get your hands stuck in to mix.

Leave the sausage mixture to sit for about 10 minutes – the onion and carrot will start to release some water and help to bind everything together. If there's not enough water to bring the flours together after 10 minutes, add 2 tablespoons of water and mix it in.

Shape the pakora mixture into 20–24 small rounds, about the size of a small meatball.

Heat enough vegetable or sunflower oil in a deep-fat fryer (if you have one) or in a heavy-based saucepan (don't fill the pan more than two-thirds full) to 180°C/350°F (or until a small piece of bread browns in 30 seconds).

Deep-fry the pakoras in batches for about 8 minutes until golden brown and crisp. Use a slotted spoon to remove them and place on kitchen paper to absorb the excess oil while you deep-fry the rest. Alternatively, to cook the pakoras in an air fryer, spray them with oil and then air-fry in batches at 180°C/350°F for 15 minutes until cooked.

To make the chutney, add all the ingredients to a blender and blend together well to form a vibrant green chutney. Serve with the warm pakoras.

CANNED TUNA

P

This snack is the epitome of elevation – taking the most basic ingredient to make the most delicious, moreish, flavour-filled bites. Although we all know Mutton Rolls (see page 63–4) will have my heart, these fish cutlets have always been a close second – crispy on the outside with moist tuna on the inside wrapped in spices and potatoes. I love how the food of my culture is so great at making undeniably tasty food with the most mundane and accessible ingredients – it's exactly how I like to cook.

FISH CUTLETS

MAKES: 10–12 **TIME: 45 MINUTES** **DIFFICULTY: 2/3**

- 2 waxy potatoes (about 300 g/ 10½ oz in total), peeled and cut into quarters
- 2 tbsp olive oil
- 2 brown onions, finely diced
- 4 garlic cloves, finely diced
- small thumb-sized piece of fresh ginger, peeled and grated
- 2 green chillies, finely diced
- 10–12 curry leaves (fresh, if available)
- 1 tsp freshly cracked black pepper
- ½ tsp ground cumin
- 2 x 125 g/4½ oz cans tuna, drained
- 2 eggs
- 100 g/3½ oz dried golden breadcrumbs
- vegetable or sunflower oil, for deep-frying
- sea salt

Add the potatoes to a saucepan with cold water that has been heavily salted. Bring to the boil and cook until fork-tender. Drain and allow to steam-dry for a few minutes before mashing the potatoes.

Meanwhile, heat the olive oil in a pan over a medium-high heat until hot, then add the onions and fry till soft, about 4 minutes. Add the garlic, ginger, chillies and curry leaves and cook for a couple of minutes, then add the black pepper and cumin and mix well.

Remove from the heat, then add the mashed potato and drained tuna. Use the handle of a wooden spoon to mix everything together. Leave the mixture to cool.

Once cool, shape the mixture into 10–12 balls.

Whisk the eggs in a bowl and place the breadcrumbs on a plate. Dip the fish balls into the egg, then into the breadcrumbs and ensure they are fully coated.

Heat enough vegetable or sunflower oil in a heavy-based saucepan so that it is deep enough to submerge the balls (but don't fill the pan more than two-thirds full). Heat to a temperature of 180°C/350°F. To check if the oil is hot enough, place a wooden spoon handle in it – it's ready to cook once it starts to bubble around the spoon.

Deep-fry the fish balls until golden brown, about 3–4 minutes, then remove to some kitchen paper using a slotted spoon to drain off the excess oil. Serve warm – I'll let you in on a trade secret, these go really well with ketchup…

GF, EF, V

Batata Harra are the spicy – and in all honesty, tastier – Lebanese cousin of Patatas Bravas. Beautifully crispy potatoes are coated in smoky flavours from Aleppo chilli flakes (pul biber) and paprika and finished with the freshness of coriander, lemon and Greek-style yogurt. I love making this to accompany fish or even to serve as a snack or canapé when we've got friends over. As you can imagine, they're gone pretty quickly.

BATATA HARRA & GARLIC YOGURT

SERVES: 4 **TIME: 1 HOUR** **DIFFICULTY: 2/3**

600 g/1 lb 5 oz **potatoes,** peeled and cut into 1.5 cm/⅝ inch cubes
5 tbsp **olive oil**
3 **garlic cloves,** finely diced
1 tsp **Aleppo chilli flakes (pul biber)**
1 tsp **paprika**
1 tbsp **tomato purée**
30 g/1 oz fresh **coriander leaves,** finely chopped
finely grated **zest of 1 lemon**
sea salt

For the garlic yogurt
120 ml/4 fl oz **Greek-style yogurt**
juice of ½ lemon
1 **garlic clove,** grated
pinch of **sea salt**
1 tsp **cracked black pepper**

Wash the potato cubes in cold water, then place in a saucepan with cold water and plenty of salt. Bring to the boil and cook until the potatoes are almost fork-tender but with a bit of a bite. Drain and set aside to steam-dry.

The potatoes can then be cooked in the oven or an air fryer. If using an oven, preheat the oven to 180°C fan/200°C/400°F/gas mark 6.

To cook them in the oven, treat them as you would roasties. Add 3 tablespoons of the olive oil to a large roasting tray and place in the oven. When the oil is hot, add the potatoes, mix around, and then roast in the oven for 40 minutes, turning a few times, until golden brown and crispy.

If using an air fryer, spread them out on a rack and spray with oil, then cook at 200°C/400°F for 20 minutes, turning halfway through, until golden brown and crispy.

While the potatoes cook, make the garlic yogurt by combining all the ingredients in a small bowl. Set aside.

So far we've just made little roasties and it's time to spice them up. Add the remaining 2 tablespoons of olive oil and garlic to a large frying pan or wok over a medium heat. Add the Aleppo chilli flakes (pul biber), paprika and tomato purée. Mix it all together. Add half of the coriander and then turn off the heat.

Once the potatoes are cooked, turn the heat back on to a high heat. Add the roasted potatoes to the pan and mix thoroughly so they are all coated.

Finish with a sprinkling of the remaining coriander and the lemon zest, then serve with the yogurt dip.

*plus cooling

These are incredibly moreish and I say that as a friendly warning. If you're making them for a group, I'd double up the recipe and hide some away for yourself the next day. It's a recipe that uses quite a few staple ingredients that you've probably already got knocking about your cupboards, making your shopping list short and sweet. This recipe is a great example of how right a mouthful can be when you balance sweet, umami, acid and fat in the perfect proportions.

CARAMELIZED ONION & MANGO CHUTNEY SAUSAGE ROLLS

MAKES: 14–16   **TIME: 1 HOUR 10 MINUTES***   **DIFFICULTY: 2/3**

1 tbsp olive oil
2 red onions, sliced
35 g/1¼ oz butter
1 tbsp light brown sugar
sea salt
100 ml/3½ fl oz boiling water
400 g/14 oz sausage meat (or sausages of your choice)
1 x 320 g/11¼ oz ready-rolled puff pastry sheet
120 g/4 oz mango chutney
6 fresh sage leaves, finely chopped
plain flour, for dusting (optional)
2 egg yolks, beaten
mixed black and white sesame seeds, for sprinkling

Add the olive oil to a frying pan with the red onions. Cook over a medium heat until the onions start to soften, then add the butter, brown sugar and a sprinkle of salt. Mix well and continue to cook until the onions caramelize, about 10 minutes. Take them off the heat and spread out on a tray to cool.

Preheat the oven to 180°C fan/200°C/400°F/gas mark 6. Line a baking tray with baking paper.

Add the sausage meat to a bowl – if you're using sausages, remove the casings and just add the meat. Combine with the cooled onions and mix together well.

Unroll the pastry sheet on to a clean, lightly floured surface, then cut it in half lengthways.

Spoon a layer of the mango chutney along the middle of each pastry strip and sprinkle the chopped sage on top. Either pipe or spoon the sausage mixture evenly on top of this layer.

Fold each strip of pastry over the filling and press down with your fingers to create a tight roll. Crimp the edges with a fork (flouring the tines of the fork beforehand will prevent it from sticking). Trim off any excess pastry from the edge of each roll.

Brush the pastry rolls with the beaten egg yolks, then sprinkle with some mixed sesame seeds.

Cut each large sausage roll into about 7–8 smaller sausage rolls. Place the small rolls, spread out, on the lined baking tray and bake in the oven for 25 minutes until cooked and golden brown. Transfer to a wire rack and serve warm.

I almost feel like these need no introduction, but a book needs words so I'll give them one. Mutton rolls are the staple of any Tamil Sri Lankan party – crispy and packed full of tender, spicy, moreish mutton. They arrive in huge cardboard boxes, arranged neatly to pack as many in as possible, and, by the time you've even considered decanting them on to a nice plate, at least half will be gone. As a kid, and frankly still to this day, if I arrive at a party after the mutton rolls have arrived, I'll forgo every greeting to find that cardboard box, and if I happen to arrive before they do, know that I'm thinking about their arrival while you're exchanging pleasantries with me. Mutton is rich and intense – compared to lamb or beef – which lends it to being wrapped in bold spices and aromatics. It can stand up to these flavours and join forces with them to create a heavenly mouthful.

MUTTON ROLLS

MAKES: 20 **TIME: 1½ HOURS*** **DIFFICULTY: 2/3**

*plus cooling

- 500 g/1 lb 4 oz mutton shoulder (or lamb shoulder), diced
- 1–2 tbsp Sri Lankan roasted curry powder (depending on spice preference)
- 2 tsp sea salt
- 2 tbsp olive oil
- 1 tsp fennel seeds
- ½ tsp black mustard seeds
- 1 brown onion, diced
- 3 green chillies, finely diced (optional)
- 10–15 curry leaves (fresh, if available)
- 1 cinnamon stick
- ½ tsp ground turmeric
- 1 tsp tomato purée

- 300 g/10½ oz Maris Piper potatoes, peeled and cut into small cubes
- 5 filo pastry sheets, quartered
- 2 eggs
- 100 g/3½ oz dried golden breadcrumbs
- sunflower oil, for deep-frying

For the spice paste
- 1 tsp fennel seeds
- ½ tsp freshly cracked black pepper
- 4 garlic cloves, peeled but left whole
- thumb-sized piece of fresh ginger, peeled and roughly chopped

Make the spice paste. Grind the fennel seeds and black pepper in a pestle and mortar. Add the garlic cloves and ginger and pound to a paste.

Add the diced mutton or lamb and the spice paste to a bowl. Add the curry powder and salt and mix well. Set aside to marinate briefly.

Heat the olive oil in a pan over a medium-high heat, then add the fennel seeds, mustard seeds and cinnamon stick. Once the mustard seeds start to spit, add the onion, chillies (if using) and curry leaves.

Once the onion has softened and coloured, about 5 minutes, add the turmeric and the marinated mutton or lamb. Give everything a good mix and cook until the meat starts to colour a bit, then add 200 ml/7 fl oz of water and the tomato purée and mix thoroughly. Cover with a lid and cook over a medium heat for about 20 minutes.

CONTINUED OVERLEAF

Add the potatoes to the curry. Add another 200 ml/7 fl oz of water and place the lid back on. Cook over a medium heat until the potatoes are soft and the curry is quite dry, about 20 minutes. Remove from the heat and leave the curry to cool for about an hour.

Place the filo pastry squares onto your work surface.

Remove the cinnamon stick from the curry. Place 2 tablespoonfuls of the curry on one corner of each filo sheet and spread out to the size of a sausage. Fold in the two sides, then fold over the top. Roll it up, enclosing the filling, and use a bit of water to dab the end edges to seal it down.

Crack the eggs into a bowl and whisk well. In another bowl or tray, add the golden breadcrumbs. Dip each filo roll into the beaten egg and coat well (getting into all the crevices), then coat in the breadcrumbs.

Heat enough sunflower oil in a deep-fat fryer (if you have one) or in a heavy-based saucepan (don't fill the pan more than two-thirds full) to 180°C/350°F (or until a small piece of bread browns in 30 seconds).

Deep-fry the filo rolls in batches until golden brown and crispy, about 3–5 minutes per batch. Using a slotted spoon, transfer the fried rolls to kitchen paper to absorb the excess oil, while you cook the rest in the same way.

Let them cool slightly before serving, and enjoy!

P

I feel strongly that sardines are widely underrated in today's society. They get overlooked for the more exciting, expensive seafood found on the fish counter, but they're great at taking on flavour and stand up to a whole load of cooking techniques. This recipe is one of those techniques and results in a delicious, crispy, fishy snack that's perfect when dunked in a chimichurri aioli.

BUTTERFLY SARDINE MILANESE WITH CHIMICHURRI AIOLI

SERVES: 10   **TIME: 40 MINUTES**   **DIFFICULTY: 2/3**

120 g/4 oz plain flour
1 tsp sea salt
good crack of black pepper
2 eggs
100 g/3½ oz panko breadcrumbs
10 g/¼ oz fresh (curly) parsley, finely chopped
finely grated zest of 1 lemon
1 tsp paprika
30 g/1 oz Parmesan cheese, finely grated
10 sardines, cleaned and cut into fillets (ask your fishmonger to do this)
sunflower oil, for shallow-frying (optional)

For the chimichurri aioli
1 egg
½ tsp Dijon mustard
3½ tsp red wine vinegar
1 garlic clove, peeled and grated
200 ml/7 fl oz olive oil
1 shallot, finely diced
1 red chilli, finely diced
10 g/¼ oz fresh (curly) parsley, finely chopped
10 g/¼ oz fresh coriander leaves, finely chopped
finely grated zest and juice of 1 lime
good pinch of sea salt

Start by making the chimichurri aioli. There are a few ways to do this, but I find using a stick blender and beaker works best. Add the egg, mustard, ½ teaspoon of the red wine vinegar and grated garlic to the beaker and blend for a few seconds to roughly incorporate everything.

With the blender left in the beaker, gently pour in the olive oil. Start the blender again, gently working your way up the beaker and you'll be left with a lovely, thick mayonnaise-like consistency (see Cook's Tip, overleaf).

Add the shallot, chilli, parsley and coriander to a bowl along with the lime zest and juice, the remaining 3 teaspoons of red wine vinegar, salt and the aioli you've just made. Mix well, then set aside.

Next, move on to the sardines. Set up three small trays or bowls. Add the flour, salt and black pepper to one tray/bowl and give it a good mix. Add the eggs to the next one and whisk. In the last one, add the panko breadcrumbs, parsley, lemon zest, paprika and grated Parmesan and use your hands to mix it all together.

CONTINUED OVERLEAF

One by one, coat the sardines in the seasoned flour, then in the eggs and finally in the breadcrumb mixture to coat.

The sardines can be shallow-fried or air-fried. I find the results in the air fryer are actually really similar to shallow-frying for this recipe. If shallow-frying, add about 1 cm/½ inch of sunflower oil to a frying pan over a medium-high heat. Once the oil is hot (when it starts to bubble when you put a wooden spoon handle in it), add the sardines (in batches) and cook for 2 minutes on each side until golden brown. Using a slotted spoon or fish slice, transfer them to some kitchen paper to absorb the excess oil, then cook the remaining sardines in the same way.

If you're using an air fryer, place them on a rack and spray with oil. Cook at 200°C/400°F for 10 minutes, turning halfway through. You may need to do this in batches depending on the size of your air fryer.

Serve the fried sardines with the chimichurri aioli to accompany.

COOK'S TIP → If you're feeling a bit lazy, simply grate or pound the garlic to a paste and add it to 200 ml/7 fl oz of mayonnaise to make your basic aioli! Then continue as above, adding the flavourings.

This is like the better-looking, funnier and annoyingly-good-at-all-sports brother of bog-standard calamari. The buttery heat is addictive to say the least and absolutely delicious. Traditionally, cuttlefish would be used for this recipe, but it's not that easy to access in the UK, so squid works as a great alternative. This is a great beer snack, but be sure to make plenty because they won't last long.

HOT BUTTER SQUID

SERVES: 4–6 **TIME: 35 MINUTES** **DIFFICULTY: 2/3**

4 squid, about 750 g/1 lb 10 oz in total, cleaned (ask your fishmonger to do this)
1 egg, beaten
juice of ½ lime
sunflower oil, for frying
60 g/2¼ oz butter
1 tsp chilli flakes
10 spring onions, each cut in half lengthways and then into 2.5 cm/1 inch pieces (keep the white and green parts separate)
2 Romano peppers, deseeded and cut into rings
6 dried whole red chillies, cut in half and seeds discarded
sea salt and freshly cracked black pepper

For the coating
120 g/4 oz cornflour
30 g/1 oz plain flour
2 tsp salt
2 tsp freshly cracked black pepper
2 tsp Sri Lankan roasted curry powder
½ tsp ground turmeric

Cut one side of each squid's body to open it up into a flat piece. Thinly score it – hold a sharp knife at a 45-degree angle and glide along the squid in a criss-cross pattern. Then cut the flat body in half lengthways and into 3 cm/1¼ inch-long rectangles.

Combine the beaten egg, lime juice and some salt and black pepper in a large bowl, then add the prepped squid to the bowl and turn to coat all over.

In a separate large bowl, combine all the coating ingredients and mix well.

Add the squid to the coating mix and turn over, making sure it's well coated all over, then set aside.

Add enough sunflower oil to a saucepan so it's about 4 cm/1½ inches deep, and place over a medium-high heat. Once the oil is hot (it starts to bubble when you put a wooden spoon handle in it), fry the squid in batches. They'll only need a minute or two each and will turn to a golden-yellow colour. Using a slotted spoon or spider strainer, transfer the cooked squid to kitchen paper to absorb the excess oil, and set aside while you cook the rest.

Place a wok over a high heat. Once hot, add the butter and chilli flakes. Once the butter starts to foam, add the spring onion whites and stir-fry for 30 seconds. Add the fried squid and the pepper rings. Toss everything a few times so it all gets coated in the spicy butter. Add the spring onion greens and dried red chillies and cook for another couple of minutes, tossing every now and then. Serve immediately.

EF

Pork ribs are everything I look for in an ingredient – they are relatively inexpensive, they love to be elevated by bold flavours and there's absolutely no airs or graces when you get stuck into them. This recipe takes some time but it's not too much effort and it creates a real treat for a lazy Sunday or a summery barbecue. The sweet and sour mango flavours complement the pork to create an interesting alternative to pork and apples.

SPICY MANGO PORK RIBS

SERVES: 2 **TIME: 4 HOURS** **DIFFICULTY: 2/3**

500 g/1 lb 2 oz pork ribs
3 tbsp Dijon mustard

For the dry rub
1½ tbsp paprika
1 tbsp onion powder
1 tbsp garlic powder
2 tbsp light brown sugar
½ tbsp sea salt
2 tsp dried thyme
½ tsp ground cinnamon

For the glaze
1 ripe mango, peeled, stoned and roughly chopped
3 garlic cloves, peeled but left whole
2.5 cm/1 inch piece of fresh ginger, peeled
1 red chilli
2 tbsp soft brown sugar
2 tbsp light soy sauce
2 tbsp apple cider vinegar
1 tbsp tomato ketchup

Preheat the oven to 130°C fan/150°C/300°F/gas mark 3½.

Start off by making the dry rub for the pork. Combine all the dry rub ingredients in a bowl, mixing well.

Prep the pork ribs by flipping them and removing the thin layer of sinew that runs along the back.

Rub the Dijon mustard all over the pork, as this will act as a binder, then sprinkle over the dry rub. It should completely coat the ribs. You can pat the dry rub down on the ribs but don't rub it!

Wrap the seasoned pork in foil, then place in a roasting tray and cook in the oven for 3 hours until juicy and tender.

Meanwhile, to make the glaze, add all the ingredients to a blender and blend until smooth and combined. Pass this through a sieve into a saucepan. Heat over a medium-high heat until it darkens a bit and slightly thickens to a sticky glaze, about 5 minutes. Set aside.

After 3 hours, remove the pork from the oven and uncover it. Increase the oven temperature to 200°C fan/220°C/425°F/gas mark 7.

Spread the glaze over the pork ribs then pop them back in the oven for a further 15–20 minutes until deep and sticky. Alternatively, you can pop the glazed pork ribs under a hot grill or on a barbecue to finish them, or stick them in a preheated air fryer at 200°C/400°F for 5 minutes to finish. Tuck in and enjoy!

HEARTY COMFORT

*plus marinating

I think we all need a few one-tray wonders in our back pocket for those tough days when cooking is the last thing you can muster up the energy for, but you know that a decent meal is the one thing your mind and body needs. I love using East Asian flavours to elevate simple, cheap ingredients like chicken and rice. From heat to sweetness and acid to umami, they bring in all the flavour profiles to make simple food utterly scrumptious.

KOREAN CHICKEN & RICE

SERVES: 4–6 **TIME: 50 MINUTES*** **DIFFICULTY: 2/3**

- 80 ml/2½ fl oz light soy sauce
- 3 tbsp gochujang
- 2 tbsp rice wine vinegar
- 2 tbsp honey
- 1 kg/2 lb 4 oz chicken thighs, skin-on, bone-in
- 2 tsp sesame oil
- 4 spring onions, thinly sliced
- 3 garlic cloves, minced
- 400 g/14 oz basmati rice, washed and drained
- 200 g/7 oz Tenderstem broccoli, stems chopped into small pieces, florets reserved separately
- 2 red peppers, deseeded and diced
- sea salt

To finish
- 1 tbsp sesame seeds
- sriracha, for drizzling (optional)
- kewpie mayonnaise, for drizzling (optional)

Combine the soy sauce, gochujang, rice wine vinegar and honey in a large bowl and mix well, then stir in the chicken thighs to coat them in marinade. Cover and leave to marinate in the refrigerator for at least a couple of hours, or overnight if possible.

Add the sesame oil to a Dutch oven or large casserole dish over a medium-high heat, then add 3 of the spring onions and the garlic. Season with a sprinkle of salt. Once they start to colour and become fragrant, about 4 minutes, add the marinated chicken thighs, skin-side down.

Turn the thighs after about 5 minutes (not letting the skin burn) and let them cook for a few minutes on the other side before transferring them back to the marinade in the bowl.

Add the rice, chopped broccoli stems and red peppers to the pan. Mix everything together well, then add 800 ml/1½ pints of water.

Place the chicken thighs on top and brush or pour the remaining marinade over each thigh.

Cover and bring to the boil over a high heat, then turn down to low and cook for 10 minutes, or until the rice is just cooked.

Uncover, sprinkle with the broccoli florets and cover and cook on low for a final 5 minutes.

Sprinkle over the remaining spring onion, the sesame seeds and a drizzle of sriracha and kewpie mayo if you like, then serve!

EF

*plus marinating

I strongly believe fruits belong in savoury dishes when used correctly. We all know apples and pork go hand in hand, but there are so many more options than a heap of apple sauce with your pork belly roast. The apple in this dish asserts its authority early on, becoming a firm pillar of flavour in the development of the satay sauce. It elevates both the pork and the sauce by adding sweetness and sourness to the dish, which greatly benefits from both flavours. There's also something very self-righteous about swapping out a teaspoon or two of sugar for some fruit. Who knew you could get one of your five-a-day from satay pork?

APPLE SATAY PORK

SERVES: 4   **TIME: 50–80 MINUTES**   **DIFFICULTY: 2/3**

For the pork
- 550 g/1 lb 4 oz pork belly, cut into 2 cm/¾ inch cubes
- 3 garlic cloves, grated
- 2.5 cm/1 inch piece of fresh ginger, grated
- 2 tbsp mild curry powder
- 2 tsp chilli flakes
- 4 tbsp light soy sauce
- 2 tsp fish sauce
- 1 tsp sesame oil
- 1 tsp sunflower oil

For the sauce
- 2 tbsp sunflower oil
- 1 brown onion, diced
- 3 garlic cloves, grated
- 2.5 cm/1 inch piece of fresh ginger, grated
- 1 tsp chilli flakes
- 2 Granny Smith apples, cored and grated (no need to peel)
- 2 tbsp crunchy peanut butter
- 1 tbsp light soy sauce
- 1 tsp fish sauce
- 200 ml/7 fl oz coconut milk

Add the pork belly cubes to a large mixing bowl. Add the garlic and ginger, along with the curry powder, chilli flakes, soy sauce, fish sauce, sesame oil and sunflower oil and mix well to coat the pork. Leave the pork to marinate in the refrigerator for at least 30 minutes, but overnight is best.

The pork can be roasted in the oven or an air fryer. If using the oven, preheat the oven to 180°C fan/200°C/400°F/gas mark 6.

Transfer the marinated pork mixture to a roasting tin and roast in the oven for 1 hour, stirring every 15 minutes, until cooked and tender. Alternatively, use an air fryer and cook at 170°C/350°F for 30 minutes, stirring every 10 minutes, until cooked and tender.

Meanwhile, for the sauce, add the sunflower oil to a saucepan over a medium-high heat. Once it's hot, add the onion, garlic, ginger and chilli flakes. Once the onion starts to colour, add the grated apples and cook over a medium heat to allow the apples to soften and slightly caramelize, about 5 minutes.

Add the peanut butter, soy sauce and fish sauce and mix well so everything becomes a paste, then go in with the coconut milk and 200 ml/7 fl oz of water. Leave this to simmer over a medium heat for 20 minutes.

Once you have a thick sauce, stir in the hot cooked pork. Serve on steaming hot rice.

EF *plus marinating

I've said it before, I'll say it again. Fruit belongs in savoury dishes (to an extent) and this traditional Korean dish, Bulgogi, is testament to that statement. Pears aren't just used for flavour, if you have time to let the meat marinate, then the pears help to tenderize the meat too, as well as adding some sweetness and acidity. I've combined this classic Korean dish with steaming white rice and a fresh cucumber salad.

BULGOGI BOWL & CUCUMBER SALAD

SERVES: 2–4   **TIME: 30 MINUTES**   **DIFFICULTY: 2/3**

450 g/1 lb ribeye steak
1 brown onion, sliced
2 spring onions, sliced on the diagonal
1 tbsp sesame seeds
1 tbsp olive oil

For the marinade
1 **pear**, cored and chopped into small chunks (no need to peel)
4 **garlic cloves**, peeled but left whole
2 cm/1 inch piece of fresh ginger, peeled and roughly chopped
3 spring onions, roughly chopped
4 tbsp light soy sauce
2 tbsp light brown sugar
2 tsp sesame oil
1 tbsp gochujang
2 tbsp rice wine vinegar

For the cucumber salad
1 cucumber
1 garlic clove, grated
1 tsp crispy chilli oil or chilli flakes
2 tbsp rice wine vinegar
1 tbsp sesame seeds

Wrap the steak in clingfilm and place in the freezer for about 10 minutes while you prep the marinade.

Add all the marinade ingredients to a food processor and blitz together until completely combined.

Slice the chilled beef into thin strips and add to a bowl with the marinade, sliced onion, spring onions and sesame seeds. Mix well, then cover and leave to marinate in the refrigerator overnight (or for at least a couple of hours).

To make the cucumber salad, bash the cucumber with a rolling pin, then chop it into random-sized chunks. Add it to a separate bowl with the garlic, chilli oil or chilli flakes and rice wine vinegar and mix together.

Toast the sesame seeds in a small dry frying pan over a low-medium heat for about 4 minutes, then sprinkle them over the cucumber salad. Set aside.

Place a large frying pan over a high heat and add the olive oil. Once it's hot, add the marinated steak, along with the onion and spring onions, and fry over a high heat. Keep moving everything around so it doesn't burn. It should only take about 5 minutes to cook and the meat will take on a rich brown colour.

Serve with the cucumber salad and steaming hot rice.

SQUASH

EF

This lovely autumnal dish combines convenience, freshness and flavour with minimal washing up. The bulk of the dish comes together in one tray which also means all the flavours spend time building layers and coming together. It's warming and comforting and reheats easily for a tasty lunch the next day. Roasting butternut squash is a handy way to release some of its natural sweetness while creating nutty undertones that end up permeating the whole dish.

SPICY SQUASAGE ORZO TRAY

SERVES: 4 **TIME: 1 HOUR** **DIFFICULTY: 1/3**

½ butternut squash, peeled, deseeded and cut into 2 cm/ ¾ inch cubes
4 spicy or other pork sausages
1 tsp fennel seeds
1 tsp paprika
1 tsp chilli flakes (more or less depending on spice preference)
10 fresh sage leaves, torn
glug of olive oil
300 g/10½ oz orzo
500 ml/18 fl oz chicken stock
handful of pine nuts
100 g/3½ oz feta cheese, crumbled
sea salt

For the dressing
20 g/¾ oz fresh parsley
2 tbsp red wine vinegar
finely grated zest and juice of 1 lime
2 tbsp olive oil

Preheat the oven to 180°C fan/200°C/400°F/gas mark 6.

Add the squash cubes to a roasting tray. Squeeze the sausage meat out of the skins and break it into little bits, then add them to the tray, along with the fennel seeds, paprika, chilli flakes, sage, a glug of olive oil and a healthy sprinkling of salt. Mix everything together – get your hands stuck in.

Roast in the oven for 25 minutes until browned.

Add the orzo to the roasting tray and mix well, then pop back in the oven for 5 minutes.

Stir in the chicken stock and return to the oven for about 20 minutes or until the orzo is just cooked.

Meanwhile, make the dressing. Add the parsley, red wine vinegar, lime zest and juice and olive oil to a small blender and blend to a vibrant green dressing. Set aside.

Toast the pine nuts in a small dry frying pan over a low-medium heat, constantly moving them until slightly darkened, about 4 minutes.

Once the orzo is cooked, finish the dish with the crumbled feta, toasted pine nuts and your vibrant green salsa dressing. Tuck in and enjoy!

This recipe ticks so many boxes – it's quick, it's delicious, it's a little bit naughty, it's indulgent and it's like a comfort blanket in a bowl. I know you should never mess with a Carbonara but I simply cannot help myself. The umami spice brought by gochujang gives this dish a little bit of fire but a whole lot of depth. I truly think this could replace your current go-to quick dinner.

UDON GOCHU CARBONARA

SERVES: 2   **TIME: 25 MINUTES**   **DIFFICULTY: 1/3**

200 g/7 oz guanciale or smoked bacon lardons
splash of olive oil
1 egg
2 egg yolks
50 g/1¾ oz Pecorino Romano cheese, finely grated (plus extra to serve)
1–2 tbsp gochujang (depending on how spicy you like it)
450 g/1 lb straight-to-wok udon noodles
sea salt

If you're using guanciale, cut it into small cubes. Add the guanciale or lardons to a frying pan with the olive oil and cook over a low-medium heat to render the fat and make them a bit crispy. This'll take about 10 minutes and you'll have to stir it occasionally.

Meanwhile, whisk the egg and egg yolks together in a heatproof mixing bowl. Add the Pecorino and gochujang and mix everything together. Set aside.

Add boiling water to a medium saucepan and season well with salt. Add the udon noodles to the water until they separate and heat through (only a few minutes), then remove them with a pasta spoon/fork or spider strainer and add straight to the guanciale or lardons in the pan, along with 2 tablespoons of the udon cooking water, then take the frying pan off the heat. Keep the remaining hot udon water in the saucepan over a low heat.

Place the heatproof mixing bowl with the egg-gochu-peco mix over the saucepan – you now have a bain-marie! Add the noodles and guanciale/lardons to the bowl and continuously mix until you get a lovely creamy sauce. If it seems too dry, add another tablespoon of the udon water.

Serve immediately with extra cheese and enjoy.

STICKY KOREAN MEATBALLS & MISO MASH

There's flavour packed into every crevice of this hearty dish. From the aromatic ingredients that make up the meatballs, to the umami punch of miso in the mash, to the whack of flavour in the sticky glaze (which is the real star of the show), every mouthful is joyous. This is the pinnacle of indulgence and comfort, feel no guilt when you eat it, just enjoy it.

SERVES: 4   **TIME: 55 MINUTES**   **DIFFICULTY: 2/3**

For the meatballs
- 500 g/1 lb 2 oz minced pork
- 2 spring onions, finely diced (plus extra to garnish)
- 4 garlic cloves, grated
- 2 cm/1 inch piece of fresh ginger, peeled and grated
- 1 egg
- 50 g/1¾ oz panko breadcrumbs
- 1 tsp sea salt, plus extra for the potato water

For the miso mash
- 2 waxy red-skinned potatoes about 300 g/10½ oz, peeled and cut into large chunks
- 300 ml/10 fl oz double cream
- 30 g/1 oz red miso paste
- 60 g/2¼ oz cold salted butter, diced

For the glaze
- 3 tbsp honey
- 2 tbsp gochujang
- 2 tbsp light soy sauce

sesame seeds, to garnish

Preheat the oven to 180°C fan/200°C/400°F/gas mark 6.

Make the meatballs. Add the minced pork, spring onions, garlic, ginger, egg, breadcrumbs and salt to a large mixing bowl and mix well until everything is fully combined – for best results, get your hands stuck in.

Shape the mixture into about 16 golf ball-sized rough balls, then roll them between the palms of your hands to create perfect meatball shapes. Dip your hands in cold water before rolling to prevent the meatballs from sticking to your palms.

Place the meatballs in a roasting tin, then pop them in the oven for 25 minutes until cooked through.

In the meantime, make the miso mash. Heavily salt cold water in a saucepan and add the potatoes. Bring to the boil, then cook until the potatoes are fork-tender. Drain the potatoes and allow them to steam-dry while you infuse the cream.

CONTINUED OVERLEAF

Add the double cream and miso paste to a separate saucepan and heat gently. Whisk the mixture intermittently to help incorporate the miso. Once the miso has fully dissolved, strain the mixture through a sieve to remove any lumps.

Mash the potatoes and add back to the saucepan over a low heat. Pour half the miso-cream mixture into the mashed potatoes and mix well. Keep adding the miso cream until you reach your desired mash consistency. Any remaining cream can be discarded. Add the cold butter and mix well. Turn off the heat.

For the glaze, add the honey, gochujang and soy sauce to a small saucepan over a low-medium heat, then whisk until thick and glossy.

Pour the glaze over the cooked meatballs and coat well.

Slap some of the miso mash on to each plate and tower on the meatballs in the sticky glaze. Sprinkle with sesame seeds and spring onions to garnish and tuck in!

*plus marinating

This, for me, is one of the most exciting recipes in the book. It screams Friday night dinner, treat yourself and we're gonna need more napkins, all at the same time. The chicken is crispy on the outside but juicy on the inside and lathered in the glossiest sauce that dances unstoppably on your palate. Tamarind is rarely used in cooking outside of South East Asia, but I do feel it has the ability to enhance cuisines from all over the world. These chicken burgers are a fantastic example of that. Be sure to serve them with the Curry Leaf Slaw on page 16 for best results.

STICKY TAMARIND CHICKEN BURGERS

SERVES: 4 **TIME: 1 HOUR 5 MINUTES*** **DIFFICULTY: 2/3**

4 chicken thighs, filleted (see page 208)
1 quantity of Curry Leaf Slaw (see page 16)
sunflower oil, for frying (optional)
2 tbsp mayonnaise
4 brioche buns, cut in half

For the buttermilk marinade
560 ml/19 fl oz buttermilk
2 tsp garlic powder
2 tsp onion granules
2 tsp paprika
2 tsp sea salt
1 tsp freshly cracked black pepper

For the tamarind glaze
3 tbsp tamarind paste
4 tbsp light soy sauce
3 tbsp soft brown sugar
2 tbsp tomato ketchup
1 tbsp sriracha

For the crispy coating
120 g/4 oz plain flour
120 g/4 oz cornflour
2 tsp garlic powder
2 tsp onion granules
2 tsp paprika
2 tsp ground fennel
1 tsp ground turmeric
1 tsp sea salt
1 tsp freshly cracked black pepper

Add all the buttermilk marinade ingredients to a bowl, mix well, then submerge the prepped chicken thigh fillets in the marinade. Refrigerate overnight or for at least a few hours.

For the tamarind glaze, combine all the ingredients in a small saucepan and set aside for now.

In a tray or bowl, combine all the crispy coating ingredients, mixing everything together well.

Remove the chicken thigh fillets from the buttermilk marinade (discard the marinade) and let them drip a bit before adding them to the crispy coating mix, one by one. Make sure they are fully coated, patting and squeezing them to get the coating mix into every crevice.

The chicken thighs can now be shallow-fried or air-fried. If shallow-frying, add about 2 cm/¾ inch of sunflower oil to a large frying pan or saucepan and heat over a medium-high heat until hot. To check the oil is ready, you can place the handle of a wooden spoon into it – if it starts bubbling around the wooden handle it's ready for cooking.

CONTINUED OVERLEAF

Carefully place the chicken thighs away from you into the hot oil (this can be done in batches, if preferred) so the oil doesn't splash on you. Cook for about 12–15 minutes, turning halfway through, until golden, crispy and cooked through.

If air-frying, spray some sprayable sunflower oil on the coated chicken fillets and air-fry at 200°C/400°F for 20 minutes, turning halfway through, until golden and crispy.

Place the tamarind glaze over a medium heat until it starts to bubble, then bubble for 1 minute. Reserve 1 tablespoon of the glaze. Brush the remaining glaze on one side of the crispy chicken fillets. You can glaze them all over if you like but be prepared for a very rich burger!

Combine the reserved glaze with the mayo to create a tamarindaise.

Toast the brioche buns on both sides under the grill or in a pan.

Build your burgers – add a layer of tamarindaise to the base of each toasted bun, followed by the glazed crispy chicken. Add a good amount of the curry leaf slaw and finally top with the other half of the bun. Serve any remaining Curry Leaf Slaw (see page 16) alongside.

This is pure indulgence – crumbly shortcrust pastry packed full of spiced tender chicken thighs. It blows any balti pie out of the water. This chicken curry was a staple in our household growing up, though unfortunately my parents never encased it in pastry, but that's probably for the best. I never viewed chicken as a boring protein because I was introduced to it surrounded by the spices and flavours in this recipe. It's a great example of how everyday ingredients, that may not necessarily sing on their own, can be elevated with the right accompaniments and processes. Serve this pie with plain or spiced mash and some roasted veg.

TAMIL CHICKEN CURRY PIE

SERVES: 6 **TIME: 1 HOUR 40 MINUTES*** **DIFFICULTY: 3/3**

- 1 kg/2 lb 4 oz chicken thighs, filleted (see page 208), skin discarded and meat cut into 2 cm/¾ inch cubes
- 4 tsp Sri Lankan roasted curry powder
- 1 tbsp Greek-style yogurt
- 1 tsp sea salt
- good crack of black pepper
- 2 tbsp sunflower oil
- ½ tsp black mustard seeds
- ½ tsp fennel seeds
- 1 brown onion, diced
- 10 curry leaves (fresh, if available)
- 4 garlic cloves, finely diced
- thumb-sized piece of fresh ginger, finely diced
- 1 tsp ground turmeric
- 3 ripe tomatoes, cut into sixths
- 200 ml/7 fl oz coconut milk

For the pastry
- 400 g/14 oz plain flour, plus extra for dusting
- 200 g/7 oz cold butter, diced
- 2 tsp sea salt
- 3–4 tbsp ice-cold water
- 1 egg yolk
- 50 ml/2 fl oz double cream

Add the chicken cubes to a bowl with 2 teaspoons of the curry powder, the yogurt, salt and black pepper. Mix well and set aside for 30 minutes.

Add the sunflower oil to a pan along with the mustard and fennel seeds over a medium-high heat. When the mustard seeds start to spit, add the onion, curry leaves, garlic and ginger and cook until the onion is translucent, about 4 minutes.

Add the remaining 2 teaspoons of curry powder and the turmeric. Give everything a good mix, then add the tomatoes and the marinated chicken.

Stir in the coconut milk and cook over a medium-high heat for about 20 minutes until it's deep in colour and the sauce is thick. Remove from the heat and leave to cool completely.

CONTINUED OVERLEAF

Meanwhile, make the pastry. Tip the flour and cold butter into a bowl and rub together between your fingertips to get a breadcrumb-like texture. Stir in the salt, then add enough ice-cold water to bring the dough together fully.

Turn it out on to a surface and knead it slightly to make a ball, then flatten into a thick disc, wrap in clingfilm and refrigerate for at least 30 minutes.

Preheat the oven to 180°C fan/200°C/400°F/gas mark 6.

Roll out the pastry on a lightly floured surface until it's about 5 mm/¼ inch thick, then cut off a section (about a third) big enough to top the pie and set it aside. Use the rest of the pastry to line the inside of a 15 cm/6 inch pie tin. Fill with the cool chicken curry, then top with the remaining pastry.

Trim and crimp the edges and poke a hole in the middle for steam to escape.

Whisk together the egg yolk and double cream, then brush this over the pie.

Bake in the oven for 40–50 minutes until the pastry is cooked and golden brown. Leave the pie to cool a little before tucking in.

EF

This is my idea of a perfect Sunday, spending a bit of time in the afternoon prepping a delicious dinner for the evening. What I love about this ragù is that it can be used in so many ways – cook some rigatoni and fold through the shredded ox cheeks, serve it atop the Celeriac and Saffron Risotto on page 141, or simply dollop it on top of creamy mash, or enjoy it eaten for lunch the next day on a slice of toasted sourdough. The chocolate and chilli add a whole level of complexity, depth and a little heat. The ox cheek is slow cooked so it has plenty of time to take on these wonderful flavours and transforms itself from something quite tasty but slightly boring to a delicious, exciting and interesting dish.

CHOCOCHILLI OX CHEEK RAGÙ

SERVES: 4–6 **TIME: 3½–4 HOURS** **DIFFICULTY: 3/3**

1 kg/2 lb 4 oz ox cheeks
1 tbsp olive oil
1 brown onion or 1 banana shallot, diced
1 carrot, diced
2 celery sticks, diced
300 ml/10 fl oz red wine
1 bay leaf

1 large sprig of fresh rosemary
4 sprigs of fresh thyme
500 ml/18 fl oz beef stock
1–2 tbsp gochujang or doubanjiang (or use 1–2 red chillies, finely chopped), depending on your spice preference

25 g/1 oz dark chocolate
sea salt and freshly cracked black pepper

COOK'S TIP → I used a cartouche and a lid in this recipe – the cartouche's role is to ensure the liquid rolls over the meat at the top and will prevent any discolouration/toughening of meat that is poking above the liquid line, and then the lid just acts as a lid. A cartouche still allows some moisture to be lost but I'd like to minimize that here as this is quite a long cook.

Preheat the oven to 150°C fan/170°C/340°F/gas mark 3½.

Pat the ox cheeks dry and season all over with salt and black pepper.

Place a Dutch oven or large casserole dish over a medium-high heat and add the olive oil. Once it's hot, add the ox cheeks and allow them to get a good sear on each side, then remove from the pan.

Add the diced vegetables to the pan and cook over a medium-high heat until softened and darkened in colour, about 10 minutes. Sprinkle with some salt.

Add the red wine and cook until reduced by half.

Meanwhile, make a bouquet garni with the bay leaf, rosemary and thyme (see page 206).

Add the beef stock and the gochujang or doubanjiang (or chopped chillies) to the pan and mix well. Return the ox cheeks to the pan along with the bouquet garni. If the cheeks aren't fully submerged, add some water until they are just covered.

Make a cartouche (see page 214) and place it so it is in contact with the liquid in the pan, then cover with the lid (see Cook's Tip). Pop in the oven for 3 hours. If the cheeks are still a bit tough, return to the oven for another hour to cook until they easily pull apart. Remove the bouquet garni.

Place the pan on the hob over a low heat. Add the chocolate and mix everything together well. By this point, the ox cheeks will just break down with a spoon and spread among the sauce. Once the chocolate is melted and well incorporated, you're good to serve.

MACARONI

EF

All the hearty naughtiness of a classic mac 'n' cheese but with the moreish, spicy flavours of a coconut sambal. The sambal is folded through the pasta as well as topping it with a spicy crust. Sambal was always a staple in our household, as it's a great accompaniment for most Tamil Sri Lankan dishes but especially string hoppers and egg hoppers. Growing up, I'd begun stirring it through all sorts of dishes and realized it elevated anything you put it in, be it a sandwich or a bowl of noodles, and that's what gave me the idea for this number.

SAMBAL MAC 'N' CHEESE

SERVES: 4 **TIME: 1 HOUR** **DIFFICULTY: 2/3**

- 100 g/3½ oz desiccated coconut
- 1 tbsp boiling water
- 3 tsp medium chilli powder
- 3 tsp sea salt
- 1 red onion, finely diced
- 20 g/¾ oz fresh coriander leaves, finely chopped
- juice of 2 limes
- 250 g/9 oz dried macaroni
- 60 g/2¼ oz butter
- 60 g/2¼ oz plain flour
- 600 ml/1 pint whole milk
- 150 g/5½ oz Cheddar cheese, grated, plus a little extra for the top
- 25 g/1 oz Parmesan cheese, finely grated, plus a little extra for the top

Preheat the oven to 180°C fan/200°C/400°F/gas mark 6.

Add the desiccated coconut to a bowl with the boiling water. Mix well, cover and leave for 5 minutes.

Meanwhile, add the chilli powder and salt to a pestle and mortar and grind to a fine powder.

Add the red onion and coriander to the desiccated coconut along with the chilli salt powder and the lime juice. Mix well and set aside.

Cook the macaroni in a pan of boiling water until al dente, then drain and set aside.

Place a large saucepan over a medium heat and add the butter. Let it melt and then turn to a very slightly brown colour – this will bring out a nutty flavour. Once the butter is ready, turn down the heat to low, stir in the flour and mix well – you're looking for a wet sand-like consistency.

Gradually add the milk, stirring constantly, and cook until the sauce is thickened and smooth, then simmer for a couple of minutes. Now go in with both cheeses and stir over a low heat until they have melted.

Add about two-thirds of the coconut sambal mixture to the cheese sauce along with the cooked macaroni. Stir everything together until it's all evenly mixed in.

Pour everything into an ovenproof dish and top with the remaining coconut sambal mixture and an extra grating of Cheddar and Parmesan.

Bake in the oven for 30 minutes until golden and bubbling, then rest for 10 minutes before serving.

GF, EF, V, Ve

This tomato curry is simple to make but is so complex in its layers of flavours, just like many Tamil Sri Lankan dishes. I love dishes that make the simplest ingredients the stars of the show – the slight sweetness of tomatoes is balanced out by the tang of tamarind, creaminess of coconut, all the aromatics and as much or as little spice as you like. Tomatoes are humble, cheap and accessible but pack so much potential. They range in taste with the seasons and vary by variety, meaning this curry develops subtle differences every time you make it – rich and deep in late summer but slightly brighter and sharper in early spring. These humble ingredients not only give us great bases for flavour but they also change and keep us on our (tomat)toes. Mop up this curry with bread or parathas, or serve it on steaming hot rice.

THAKALI KULAMBU

SERVES: 2–4 TIME: 20 MINUTES DIFFICULTY: 1/3

1 tbsp sunflower oil
½ tsp black mustard seeds
½ tsp cumin seeds
4 small round shallots, peeled and cut in half
6 garlic cloves, cut into strips
10 curry leaves (fresh, if available)
2 bird's eye chillies, cut in half (optional)
pinch of sea salt
¼ tsp fenugreek seeds

1–2 tsp Sri Lankan roasted curry powder (depending on spice preference)
½ tsp ground turmeric
6 ripe tomatoes, each cut into 8 wedges
2 tsp tamarind paste
150 ml/5 fl oz coconut milk

Add the sunflower oil to a large pan and heat over a high heat until hot, then add the mustard and cumin seeds.

When the mustard seeds start to spit, add the shallots, garlic, curry leaves and chillies (if using). Season with the pinch of salt and mix, then cook for a few minutes.

Add the fenugreek seeds, curry powder and turmeric. Mix well, then add the tomatoes and tamarind paste. Cook over a medium-high heat for a few minutes, then add 300 ml/10 fl oz of water and the coconut milk and bring to a simmer. Leave to simmer for 15 minutes to build some depth into the sauce. Season to taste.

Serve with rice or flatbreads of your choice.

EF

As winter warmers go, it doesn't get much more comforting than this. Layers of slow-cooked duck leg ragù, sandwiched between a creamy béchamel and lovely sheets of pasta. Get this cooking after a slow and lazy Sunday morning and enjoy the fruits of your labour for dinner that evening. Classic lasagnes are great but the slowly braised duck leg adds a hint of gamey sweetness to this well-loved dish.

DUCK LEG LASAGNE

SERVES: 5–6 **TIME: 4½–5 HOURS** **DIFFICULTY: 3/3**

4 duck legs, skin-on
1 carrot, diced
2 brown onions, diced
2 celery sticks, diced
300 ml/10 fl oz red wine
500 ml/18 fl oz beef stock
400 g/14 oz can chopped tomatoes
½ tsp chilli flakes (optional)
2 bay leaves
400 g/14 oz dried lasagne sheets
sea salt and freshly cracked black pepper

For the béchamel sauce
75 g/2¾ oz butter
75 g/2¾ oz plain flour
750 ml/26 fl oz whole milk
75 g/2¾ oz Parmesan cheese, finely grated, plus an extra 25 g/1 oz

CONTINUED OVERLEAF

Preheat the oven to 150°C fan/170°C/340°F/gas mark 3½.

Season the duck legs with salt and black pepper, then add them to a cold Dutch oven or large casserole dish, skin-side down. Heat over a medium heat to render some of the fat in the skin and to give them a nice, brown colour. Turn the legs over and colour the rest of the meat. Remove the legs from the pan when they are seared all over.

Add the carrot, onion and celery (soffritto) to the pan and give it a good mix to release all the flavour from the bottom of the pan that the duck legs left behind.

Once the veg has started to soften, add the red wine and allow this to reduce by half. Stir in the beef stock, canned tomatoes and chilli flakes (if using). Return the duck legs to the pan along with the bay leaves.

Cover with a cartouche (optional – see page 214) and place the lid on the pan. Transfer to the oven and cook for 3 hours until the duck meat is very tender.

Make the béchamel *sauce*. Heat the butter in a saucepan over a medium heat until fully melted but not coloured. Add the flour and mix well, then cook until you have the consistency of wet sand.

Gradually add the milk over a low-medium heat, whisking continuously, until thickened and smooth, then simmer for a couple of minutes. Stir in 75 g/2¾ oz of the Parmesan over a low heat until melted. Set aside.

Remove the duck legs from the pan and discard the bay leaves. Shred the duck legs and discard the bones and skin. Return the shredded meat to the veg sauce and place back on the hob over a low heat.

Turn the oven up to 180°C fan/200°C/400°F/gas mark 6.

Start to assemble the lasagne in an ovenproof dish, about 30 x 20 cm/12 x 8 inches. Start with a layer of lasagne sheets, followed by some duck ragù, then some béchamel, then top with a layer of some of the remaining Parmesan. Repeat these layers until you've used up all the components, finishing with a final sprinkling of Parmesan.

Cover loosely with foil and bake in the oven for 30 minutes, then remove the foil and bake for another 15 minutes until golden and bubbling. Leave it to rest for 10 minutes before diving in.

AUBERGINES

GF, EF, V, Ve

There's always one person in a family that makes the best version of a particular dish and that's no different in mine – someone makes the best mutton curry, someone makes the best desserts (I'm giving no names here because it won't be worth the backlash...) but everyone, and I mean everyone, in our family, extended family and friends knows that my mum's fried aubergine is THE best aubergine dish around. It's requested at every event and there'd be a full-on revolt if anyone turned up to a party at our family home and there wasn't a vat of it waiting to be demolished. Mum kindly passed on the recipe to me and I to you, but there's an element of intuition that can't be written down, which makes me certain that none of us will ever be able to live up to her famous dish, but we sure can try.

AMMA'S AUBERGINE PORIYAL

SERVES: 4–6 AS A SIDE **TIME: 45 MINUTES** **DIFFICULTY: 2/3**

- 3 **aubergines,** cut into 1 cm/½ inch cubes
- **vegetable or sunflower oil,** for deep-frying
- 6 **garlic cloves,** 3 peeled and left whole, 3 grated
- 2 tbsp **olive oil**
- 1 **cinnamon stick**
- 3 **dried red chillies** (optional)
- 1½ **red onions,** finely diced
- 10–15 **curry leaves** (fresh, if available)
- 2.5 cm/1 inch piece **of fresh ginger,** grated
- ½ tsp **hot chilli powder** (or more if you like it spicy)
- 3 **tomatoes,** diced
- **sea salt** (optional)

If you sprinkle the aubergine cubes with salt to draw out a bit of moisture before frying, it can really enhance the flavour of the aubergine (see Cook's Tip on how to do this), but this is up to you.

Heat enough vegetable or sunflower oil in a deep-fat fryer (if you have one) or in a heavy-based saucepan (don't fill the pan more than two-thirds full) to 180°C/350°F (or until a small piece of bread browns in 30 seconds).

Add the aubergine cubes to the hot oil in batches and then remove them (using a slotted spoon) when the flesh turns a deep golden brown colour and the skin is shiny. Transfer them to lots of kitchen paper to soak up the excess oil, while you deep-fry the remaining batches.

When the aubergine is cooked, turn off the heat, add the whole garlic cloves to the hot oil and leave to soften and colour for 5 minutes, then add to the cooked aubergine.

Heat the olive oil in a large pan or wok over a medium-high heat, then once it's hot, add the cinnamon stick and whole dried red chillies (if using). After about 30 seconds, add the red onions and curry leaves. Give it all a decent mix and cook for a couple of minutes.

Add the grated garlic and ginger along with the chilli powder and tomatoes. Mix everything together, then add the fried aubergine cubes and whole garlic cloves. Give it a good stir and pop a lid on, then let that cook over a medium heat for about 15 minutes, stirring every 5 minutes. Plate up and enjoy!

COOK'S TIP → Sprinkle the aubergine cubes with salt and mix them thoroughly. Lay them out on clean tea towels or kitchen paper and leave them to sit for about 30 minutes. Mix them around a few times during this time. Pat them dry before you fry them.

GF, EF, P

Certain dishes are packed full of memories and this is definitely one of them. My lovely wife, Anna, taught me early on that life was for living and taking time out to travel, and that enjoying the journey was more important than anything else. She seems to do this effortlessly and it's that ethos that led us to a lovely little island in Brazil, during a three-month trip across South America, where we ate this delicious dish in a tiny restaurant on a sandy road. This ethos that Anna has instilled in me is probably the reason I'm now immersed in a career I love based purely on a passion for food. This stew is packed full of memories of that island and reminders of why living life and slowing down can actually lead to the outcome you truly want and need.

BRAZILIAN FISH STEW

SERVES: 4   **TIME: 55 MINUTES**   **DIFFICULTY: 1/3**

- 1 tbsp olive oil
- 5 garlic cloves, finely diced
- 1 brown onion, diced
- 3 red peppers, deseeded and diced
- 2 tsp paprika
- 1 tsp sea salt
- 1 tsp chilli flakes
- 1 tbsp tomato purée
- 400 ml/14 fl oz vegetable stock
- 400 ml/14 fl oz can coconut milk
- 350 g/12 oz chilled fish pie mix

Add the olive oil and garlic to a large saucepan and place over a medium-high heat. As soon as the garlic starts to slightly colour, add the onion and red peppers. Cook until the onion is soft and slightly coloured, about 10 minutes.

Add the paprika, salt and chilli flakes and mix well before adding the tomato purée.

Stir in the veg stock and coconut milk, then bring to a simmer and cook uncovered for about 30 minutes until the liquid is reduced by half.

Add the fish pie mix to the sauce and cook for a further 10 minutes.

Serve with steaming hot rice or crusty bread.

TWIST

MUSSELS

GF, EF, P

I've made many mussel-related creations – they seem to love being enveloped in lots of flavour – but I do think this is my best yet. There's definitely a nostalgia-related bias to my decision, as the flavours in this dish are influenced by the delicious Tamil fish curries my parents make. With many miles of coastline, Sri Lanka is surrounded by seafood and therefore has some of the best recipes for using it. I've taken that inspiration and moulded it around a classic French way of cooking mussels. It's a real winner, perfect when served with crusty sourdough or even a large bowl of fries.

JAFFNA MUSSELS

SERVES: 2   TIME: 40 MINUTES   DIFFICULTY: 2/3

1 kg/2 lb 4 oz mussels in shell
2 tbsp sunflower or vegetable oil
1 tsp black mustard seeds
1 tsp cumin seeds
1 brown onion, diced
10 curry leaves (fresh, if available)
1 tsp sea salt, plus extra for the mussels water
2 garlic cloves, grated
2 ripe tomatoes, chopped
¼ tsp fenugreek seeds
1 tbsp Sri Lankan roasted curry powder
½ tsp ground turmeric
200 ml/7 fl oz dry white wine
1 tsp tamarind paste
200 ml/7 fl oz coconut milk
warm crusty bread (gluten-free, if required), to serve

Prep the mussels according to the instructions on page 212.

Add the sunflower or vegetable oil to a large pan that has a lid and place over a medium heat. Add the mustard and cumin seeds, then once the mustard seeds start to spit, add the onion, curry leaves, measured salt and the grated garlic.

Cook until the onion colours and starts to soften, then go in with the chopped tomatoes, fenugreek seeds, curry powder and turmeric. Mix well and cook for a few minutes before adding the wine.

Allow the wine to reduce by about 75 per cent, then stir in the tamarind paste and coconut milk and leave to simmer for about 10 minutes.

Drain the mussels and add to the pan. Give everything one quick mix, then pop the lid on and simmer for 5 minutes until the mussels are open and cooked (discard any that haven't opened).

Ladle the mussels into bowls along with plenty of the delicious sauce and serve with warm crusty bread and extra crispy fried curry leaves.

COD FILLETS

GF (DEPENDING ON LAKSA PASTE), EF, P

The ability of oranges to lift seafood is totally underrated. They add a little hint of acidity but a huge whack of fragrance and lively flavour which seem to marry up with the bold, fragrant taste of laksa so well. This dish feels hearty and comforting but also fresh and light all at the same time. It's perfect in the depths of winter as well as on a sunny summer's evening – it's definitely one to add to your weekly recipe rotation.

CITRUS COD LAKSA

SERVES: 4 **TIME: 50 MINUTES** **DIFFICULTY: 2/3**

2 tbsp sunflower oil
120 g/4 oz laksa paste (for home-made, see recipe opposite)
400 ml/14 fl oz can coconut milk
500 ml/18 fl oz fish, vegetable or chicken stock
1 tsp fish sauce
juice of 2 oranges
juice of 2 limes
100 g/3½ oz Tenderstem broccoli, snapped into 2.5 cm/1 inch pieces
300 g/10½ oz beansprouts
4 cod fillets
chopped fresh coriander, to garnish
red chilli, to garnish

For the base mixture
2 garlic cloves, peeled but left whole
2.5 cm/1 inch piece of fresh ginger, peeled
4 small shallots or 1 brown onion, peeled
2 red bird's eye chillies

Place all the ingredients for the base mixture in a food processor or mini chopper and blend/chop together until chunky.

Add the sunflower oil to a large saucepan or Dutch oven over a medium heat. Once it's hot, add the blended/chopped base mixture and the laksa paste. Mix intermittently and cook until the colour darkens – this usually takes about 10 minutes.

Add the coconut milk, stock and fish sauce. Mix well and allow everything to simmer for about 20 minutes until the colour deepens slightly.

Stir the orange and lime juices into the sauce. Throw in the broccoli pieces along with the beansprouts.

Lay the cod fillets on top of the veg so they're just submerged in the sauce. Place the lid on top and simmer for about 5 minutes until the cod is completely cooked through.

Garnish with chopped coriander and red chilli, then serve on steaming hot sticky white rice.

LAKSA PASTE

MAKES: 120 G/4 OZ

4 garlic cloves, peeled but left whole
2.5 cm/1 inch piece of fresh ginger, peeled
1 cm/½ inch piece of galangal, peeled
2 small shallots, peeled
2–4 red bird's eye chillies (depending on your heat preference)
1 tsp ground turmeric
1 stick of lemongrass, bashed and cut into chunks
1 tbsp shrimp paste

Add all the ingredients to a small food processor and blitz together to a paste.

Use as required.

EF, V *as a side salad

By this point, I think it's clear to see I've written a book to create the 'love children' of all my favourite foods. The way I've eaten throughout my life has been a combination of my Tamil Sri Lankan background and my British European upbringing, so it's natural that the way I create recipes is a combination of these two things too. Kothu roti and panzanella – in my opinion, two of the greatest dishes on our planet – seem to come together in perfect harmony. Rotis and parathas are cheap, cheerful and versatile, commonly used as 'cutlery' to mop up wet curries and now introduced into the world of salads. This dish is especially delicious when paired with Appa's Barbecue Mutton Chops on page 173.

KOTHU PANZANELLA

SERVES: 6–8*   **TIME: 25 MINUTES**   **DIFFICULTY: 1/3**

300 g/10½ oz vine-ripened tomatoes, quartered
300 g/10½ oz cherry tomatoes (mixed colours), halved
6 tbsp olive oil
2 tbsp red wine vinegar
good pinch of flaky sea salt
hefty crack of black pepper
5 frozen rotis/parathas
½ tsp black mustard seeds
½ tsp fennel seeds
1 red onion, diced
2 green chillies, sliced (optional)
handful of curry leaves (about 20, fresh if available)

Add the vine-ripened and cherry tomatoes to a large mixing bowl. Add 4 tablespoons of the olive oil, the red wine vinegar, salt and black pepper. Mix and set aside.

Cook the rotis/parathas as directed on the packet (usually in a dry frying pan). Let them cook through completely but not colour too much as they've got some more cooking to do! Remove them from the pan, cut into 2 cm/¾ inch squares and set aside.

Add the remaining 2 tablespoons of olive oil to a wok or large frying pan over a high heat, then once the oil is hot, add the mustard and fennel seeds.

Once the mustard seeds start to spit, add the red onion, green chillies (if using) and curry leaves. After about 30 seconds, add the squares of roti/paratha. Continue to cook over a high heat, mixing regularly, for about 3–5 minutes.

Add the fried roti/paratha squares mixture to the bowl of tomatoes and mix well, then serve immediately.

COOK'S TIP → If you'd like to make this in advance, follow the method above and then just combine everything (see step 5) just before you serve. I wouldn't recommend making it much more than a few hours in advance.

GF, EF, P

This is full-on nostalgia for me – this incredibly humble curry is one of my all-time favourite childhood dinners and testing this recipe took me back like a time machine. Being a kid, I had no idea how basic an ingredient pilchards were, for all I knew they were the queens of the ocean! It's the best example in this book, and probably one of the first examples I have experienced, of true elevation of the most basic ingredient. Seems my parents were writing *Elevate* long before I was.

CANNED FISH CURRY

SERVES: 4 **TIME: 25 MINUTES** **DIFFICULTY: 2/3**

2 tbsp sunflower or vegetable oil
1 tsp black mustard seeds
1 brown onion, diced
2 green chillies, chopped (optional)
10 curry leaves (fresh, if available)
6 garlic cloves, cut into large chunks
½ tsp cumin seeds
¼ tsp fenugreek seeds
½ tsp ground turmeric
½ tbsp Sri Lankan roasted curry powder
2 x 400 g/14 oz cans pilchards in tomato sauce
200 ml/7 fl oz boiling water

Heat the sunflower or vegetable oil in a large pan over a medium-high heat and add the mustard seeds. Once they start to spit, add the onion, green chillies (if using), curry leaves and garlic.

Once the onion has coloured and softened a bit, add the cumin and fenugreek seeds and mix well. After about a minute, add the turmeric and curry powder and mix again.

Add the cans of pilchards and tomato sauce, along with the boiling water and then leave to simmer with the lid on for about 10 minutes to allow the sauce to thicken slightly.

Serve with steaming hot rice, naans, chapatis or parathas.

GF, EF

When we think of wasabi it's normal to immediately think of an unpredictable, mind-numbing paste that can blow your socks off, but using it in this way completely changes things. The wasabi fire is mellowed and you can actually enjoy the flavour it brings to a dish. The effect is similar to the addition of mustard to a creamy mash or cheesy sauce. This is a super fragrant dish and vibrant to look at, so it's a perfect weeknight dinner but also an impressive dish to serve up to guests.

WASABI CHICKEN

SERVES: 4   **TIME: 50 MINUTES**   **DIFFICULTY: 2/3**

- 2 small or 1 large brown onion(s), cut into rough chunks
- 6 garlic cloves, whole and peeled
- 2.5 cm/1 inch piece of fresh ginger, peeled and cut into rough chunks
- 1 stick of lemongrass, bashed and cut into small pieces
- 20 g/¾ oz fresh coriander leaves, plus extra to garnish
- 2 tbsp rice wine vinegar
- 1 tsp fish sauce
- 1 kg/2 lb 4 oz chicken thighs, skin-on and bone-in
- 2 tbsp sunflower oil
- 400 ml/14 fl oz can coconut milk
- handful of flaked almonds
- 2 tbsp wasabi paste
- juice of 2 limes

Add the onion(s), garlic, ginger, lemongrass, coriander, rice wine vinegar and fish sauce to a food processor and blend until you get a smooth green paste. Set aside.

Fillet the chicken thighs (see page 208) and cut the meat into roughly 2 cm/¾ inch cubes, do not discard to bones.

Add the sunflower oil to a large pan over a medium-high heat, then once it's hot, add the pieces of chicken and fry until they are coloured all over. You may need to do this in batches to avoid overcrowding the pan, otherwise the chicken will not brown. Ensure the bones are thrown in for some colour too as they'll go into the sauce to give us more flavour. Remove from the pan and set aside.

Add the green paste to the pan and cook over a medium heat for about 5 minutes while stirring. If it starts to stick, add a little more oil. Pour in the coconut milk and mix well.

Return the chicken (and bones, for flavour) to the pan, mix well and then simmer for about 15 minutes until the chicken is fully cooked and the sauce has thickened.

Meanwhile, place a small dry frying pan over a medium heat and add in the flaked almonds. Move them around intermittently to prevent burning. Once toasted, about 3–4 minutes, remove from the pan and set aside.

Turn off the heat under the chicken pan and stir the wasabi paste and lime juice into the chicken mixture. Mix well and finish with a sprinkle of extra coriander leaves and the toasted flaked almonds. Serve with steaming hot white rice.

EF, P

Dishes like this epitomize the way I love to cook – fragrant and comforting without breaking the bank or taking up your entire evening. Poaching chicken is a great way to cook it healthily while imparting flavour and preventing overcooking – after a few minutes it'll flake apart and melt in your mouth. This is definitely one to add to the quick dinner repertoire.

PEANUT BUTTER CHICKEN UDON SOUP

SERVES: 2 **TIME: 40 MINUTES** **DIFFICULTY: 1/3**

- 2 tsp sesame oil
- 4 spring onions, chopped
- 2 garlic cloves, finely diced
- 2.5 cm/1 inch piece of fresh ginger, peeled and finely diced
- ½ tsp chilli flakes
- 2 tbsp peanut butter (smooth or crunchy)
- 2 tbsp light soy sauce
- 1 tsp fish sauce
- 300 ml/10 fl oz can coconut milk
- 300 ml/10 fl oz chicken stock
- 1 stick of lemongrass, bashed
- 2 chicken breasts
- 300 g/10½ oz straight-to-wok udon noodles
- 90 g/3¼ oz mangetout, halved lengthways
- 100 g/3½ oz Tenderstem broccoli, cut into 4 cm/1 inch pieces
- handful of salted peanuts

To finish
- 1 tbsp sesame seeds
- 1 spring onion, finely sliced
- 1–2 red chillies, thinly sliced
- crispy chilli oil
- juice of 1 lime

Add the sesame oil to a pan over a medium heat and, when it's hot, add the spring onions, garlic, ginger and chilli flakes and cook for about 3 minutes until fragrant and soft.

Add the peanut butter, soy sauce, fish sauce, then pour in the coconut milk and chicken stock. Add the lemongrass stick to the pan.

Mix well, then add the chicken breasts and bring to a very gentle simmer for 15 minutes.

Remove the chicken breasts and shred them with two forks.

Add the chicken back to the broth along with udon noodles, mangetout and broccoli. Cover with a lid and cook over a low heat for 4 minutes until veg is cooked.

Meanwhile, add the peanuts to a small dry frying pan and toast over a medium heat until slightly coloured, about 4 minutes, then roughly chop.

Ladle the creamy peanutty soup into bowls, then top with the toasted peanuts, the sesame seeds, sliced spring onion, red chilli slices, crispy chilli oil and a squeeze of lime juice. Enjoy!

FIRM TOFU

EF, V, Ve

You'll probably read the title of this recipe and then delve into the ingredients and wonder whether I've had a head injury – Marmite and apple juice?! But stick with me. Marmite is a great ingredient to use in cooking, as it has all the meatiness and depth of meat-based products but none of the, well, meat. I use it in anything from slow-cooked ragùs to sticky glazes, and every now and then I'll even stick it on some toast. Apple juice is also a great ingredient for these types of dishes – it adds a sweet and acidic note to the sauce and reduces down to become glossy and sticky. Serve this as part of a spread or even just with a bowl of steaming hot rice for a quick dinner.

STICKY MARMITE TOFU

SERVES: 2   **TIME: 25–45 MINUTES**   **DIFFICULTY: 1/3**

200 g/7 oz firm tofu
1 tbsp sesame oil
1 tbsp cornflour
1 tsp sea salt
sunflower or vegetable oil, for shallow-frying (optional)

For the sauce
100 ml/7 fl oz unsweetened apple juice
2 tbsp light soy sauce
1 tbsp Marmite
1 tbsp apple cider vinegar
2 tsp sesame oil
1 tbsp cornflour
½ tsp chilli powder (optional)

To garnish
mixed black and white sesame seeds
sliced spring onions

Tear the tofu into roughly 2 cm/¾ inch pieces. Tearing is much better than cutting in this recipe because there's a larger surface area to produce more crispy bits.

Add the tofu to a bowl with the sesame oil, cornflour and salt and toss together to ensure all the pieces are evenly coated.

If you've got an air fryer, you can pop the coated tofu pieces in, spray with some oil, and cook at 200°C/400°F for 12 minutes until they're golden brown and perfectly crispy. Or you can shallow-fry them in the sunflower or vegetable oil in a frying pan over a medium-high heat for about 6 minutes, until golden brown and crispy all over. Alternatively, you can place them on a wire rack over a baking tray and bake in a preheated oven at 180°C fan/200°C/400°F/gas mark 6 for about 30 minutes.

In the meantime, make the sauce. Combine all the sauce ingredients in a saucepan and whisk together, then cook over a medium-high heat until the sauce becomes thick and sticky, stirring occasionally, about 5 minutes.

Once the tofu is cooked, add it to the sauce and mix well until every nook and cranny of the tofu is covered in the delicious sauce.

Garnish with mixed sesame seeds and a sprinkle of sliced spring onions and serve on steaming hot rice.

EF, V, Ve

This unassuming broccoli dish will be the star of the show when your guests start tucking in. The tangy tamarind brings the broccoli to life and the bold flavours are mellowed out by the smooth, comforting butter bean hummus. It's a great dish to serve as part of a spread or it's even brilliant just scooped up with toasted sourdough for a delicious lunch or dinner.

TAMARIND TENDERSTEM ON BUTTER BEAN HUMMUS

SERVES: 4 **TIME: 35 MINUTES** **DIFFICULTY: 1/3**

For the tamarind Tenderstem
- 2 tbsp tamarind paste
- 2 tbsp soft brown sugar
- 1 tbsp light soy sauce
- 2 tbsp boiling water
- 2 garlic cloves, grated
- 2.5 cm/1 inch piece of fresh ginger, peeled and grated
- ½ tsp ground cumin
- ½ tsp crushed dried red chillies
- ¼ tsp sea salt
- 200 g/7 oz Tenderstem broccoli

For the butter bean hummus
- 400 g/14 oz can butter beans, drained but liquid reserved separately
- 1 tbsp tahini
- 1 tsp white miso paste
- juice of 1 lemon
- ½ tsp sea salt
- ¼ tsp ground cumin
- 2 ice cubes

Preheat the oven to 180°C fan/200°C/400°F/gas mark 7, or preheat an air fryer to 170°C/350°F.

For the tamarind Tenderstem, combine all the ingredients, except the broccoli, in a small saucepan and mix well. Cook over a medium heat until it's thick, glossy and sticky, about 5–10 minutes.

Meanwhile, blanch the broccoli in a separate pan of boiling water for about 3 minutes, then drain and place in a bowl.

Add half the tamarind mixture to the broccoli and mix well.

Place the broccoli on a baking tray or air fryer rack and either roast in the oven for 15 minutes or cook in the air fryer for 10 minutes, until slightly charred and a bit sticky.

Meanwhile, make the hummus. Add the butter beans to a blender along with all the other hummus ingredients and blend until smooth. If the mixture seems too dry to mix, gradually blend in a little of the reserved butter bean liquid to achieve the right consistency.

Spread the hummus on a serving plate and layer up with the roasted broccoli. Finish with a healthy drizzle of the remaining tamarind mixture, and serve.

ELEVATE

GF, P

This is in no way a traditional Caponata – it's not normal to find anchovies in a caponata, let alone mustard seeds, fennel seeds and curry leaves! However, I wanted to take elements from a proper Jaffna aubergine curry and implant them into the cooking process of a classic Caponata. I think it's possible to lend flavour techniques from one culture to another without removing the original essence of the dish and instead elevating it to something just a little bit more exciting – it's a technique that forms a huge part of my creativity and cooking style. Pair this with the Fennel and Curry Leaf Focaccia on page 152 for the most deliciously comforting bowl of food you'll eat.

JAFFNA CAPONATA

SERVES: 4   **TIME: 1 HOUR**   **DIFFICULTY: 2/3**

- 2 large aubergines, cut into small cubes
- 2 tbsp olive oil, plus extra for drizzling
- 50 g/1¾ oz can anchovy fillets in olive oil
- 1 tsp black mustard seeds
- 1 tsp fennel seeds
- 20 curry leaves (fresh, if available)
- 1 red onion, finely diced
- 3 garlic cloves, finely diced
- ½–1 tsp chilli flakes (depending on your heat preference)
- 1 tbsp red wine vinegar
- 3 celery sticks, cut into small chunks
- 250 g/9 oz baby plum tomatoes, halved
- 400 g/14 oz can chopped tomatoes
- 70 g/2½ oz stoned green olives, roughly chopped
- 2 tbsp capers, drained
- 2 tbsp pine nuts
- 15 g/½ oz fresh basil leaves, roughly torn

Preheat the oven to 200°C fan/220°C/425°F/gas mark 7.

Place the aubergine cubes into a roasting tray. Drizzle a liberal amount of olive oil over and mix to make sure every cube is coated.

Roast in the oven for 30 minutes, turning halfway through, until the skin glistens and the flesh has browned.

Add 2 tablespoons of the remaining olive oil to a large saucepan over a medium heat. Add the anchovies with the oil from their can and cook until they break down, then add the mustard and fennel seeds and curry leaves. Once the seeds start to spit, add the onion, garlic and chilli flakes and mix well, then stir in the red wine vinegar.

Mix in the cooked aubergine cubes, celery chunks and baby tomatoes, then stir in the canned tomatoes along with 400 ml/14 fl oz of water. Bring to a simmer, then leave to bubble away and thicken for about 20 minutes. Add the olives and capers to the sauce.

Meanwhile, add the pine nuts to a dry frying pan. Stir over a medium-high heat until brown and toasted.

Tip the pine nuts into the caponata along with the torn basil leaves and stir to mix, then serve.

P *plus curing

I first tried cured sardines on a sunny Christmas holiday in Portugal. I'm sure the beautiful riverside Tavira scenery and the even more beautiful, pale, crisp rosé strongly influence my memories of this cured sardine dish, but it was truly one of the most sophisticated and enjoyable creations I've tasted. I love any dish that takes a simple ingredient and elevates it to a totally new realm, it's really the type of cooking that inspires this book. I immediately felt an urge to create something with cured sardines and, if you're looking to push the boat out and impress someone for breakfast, this take on eggs royale is truly unique and much cheaper than using the traditional smoked salmon.

CURED SARDINE ROYALE WITH A TARTARE HOLLANDAISE

SERVES: 4 **TIME: 50 MINUTES*** **DIFFICULTY: 3/3**

12 fresh sardines
finely grated zest of 1 lemon
juice of 2 lemons
8 eggs (at room temperature)
splash of olive oil
4 English muffins, cut in half
280 g/10 oz sun-dried tomatoes
cayenne pepper, for sprinkling
sea salt

For the tartare hollandaise
250 g/9 oz butter
3 egg yolks
1 tsp white wine vinegar
30 g/1 oz cornichons (about 10–12), drained and finely diced
30 g/1 oz capers (drained weight), finely diced
15 g/½ oz fresh tarragon, finely chopped
15 g/½ oz fresh parsley, finely chopped
10 g/¼ oz fresh dill, finely chopped

Remove the sardine heads, then run a knife along the belly to open up the fish and remove most of the bones and guts. Remove the scales, being careful not to damage the fillets (sometimes this step is easier after the curing process). You can ask your fishmonger to do all this, if you prefer!

Sprinkle a layer of salt in a small tray and sprinkle half the lemon zest on top. Lay the sardine fillets, skin-side down, on top, then sprinkle over the remaining lemon zest. Squeeze the lemon juice all over, then cover the sardines with a thick layer of salt. Wrap the tray in clingfilm and refrigerate for 20 minutes.

Meanwhile, to make the hollandaise, start by clarifying the butter. Gently melt the butter in a saucepan over a low heat. Once melted, skim off any froth from the surface, then carefully pour the layer of clear yellow fat (on top) into a bowl, leaving the milky residue behind in the pan (discard this).

Place a medium-sized saucepan over a medium heat and fill halfway with boiling water. Place a heatproof bowl on top.

CONTINUED OVERLEAF

Add the egg yolks, vinegar and a teaspoon of water from the saucepan to the bowl and whisk until the mixture is light and smooth and you can form a figure of eight in the mix. There'll be lots of bubbles in the mixture to begin with, but when it's ready these bubbles will be gone and the consistency will be smooth.

Turn off the heat and place a tea towel between the saucepan and the bowl.

Gently drip in the melted clarified butter while whisking. At this stage, it's very easy to get overexcited/bored and pour in the butter too fast. This will cause the hollandaise to split and you'll be very sad. Slowly dribble the butter in or add a little at a time, whisking continuously to fully incorporate it between additions.

Once a thick hollandaise is formed, keep it warm while you prepare everything else – the best trick is to place it in a Thermos flask or cover with clingfilm and place in your oven at its lowest setting (ideally around 60°C/140°F).

Use the medium-saucepan with hot water to poach your eggs. You want the water to be just about simmering. I don't bother with vinegar but I do season the water with salt at this stage.

Crack your eggs into ramekins, then use a spoon to swirl the water to make a very gentle whirlpool. Add the eggs to the water by lowering the ramekins into it – you can do a couple at a time as they won't stick together!

Remove the eggs after 2½ minutes and place on a tea towel to soak up any excess liquid. Sprinkle with salt to season. Repeat to poach the remaining eggs. Once the eggs are all cooked, you can place them all back in the water at the same time for 30 seconds to heat them up just before serving.

Remove the sardines from the cure and wash them thoroughly under cold water, then dry on kitchen paper. Remove any remaining bones, fins and scales, then cut them in half lengthways.

They're ready to eat, but if you'd like to crisp the skin a bit, it can be done now. Heat a frying pan over a medium heat, add the olive oil, then place the sardine fillets, skin-side down, into the pan to get them a little crispy. This will only take about a minute.

Toast the muffin halves on both sides. Place a couple of sun-dried tomatoes on each muffin half, then lay the sardine fillets on top (3 sardine fillet halves on each muffin half).

Stir in all the diced/chopped ingredients to the hollandaise sauce and mix.

Place a poached egg on each muffin half, then pour over the tartare hollandaise and finish with a dusting of cayenne pepper. Tuck in and enjoy!

GF, EF, V, Ve

Celeriac doesn't get used in curries and after making this I really don't know why. Roasting celeriac, like many root vegetables, brings out a lovely sweetness which seems to marry up perfectly with the slight heat from this curry. The earthiness of celeriac makes for a lovely rustic dish and I love taking the celeriac a tiny bit further and creating some char when it's in the oven to accentuate that rusticity. The texture isn't dissimilar to a potato curry, but the flavour celeriac brings seems more powerful and a lot more interesting.

ROASTED CELERIAC & CHICKPEA CURRY

SERVES: 4 **TIME: 1 HOUR** **DIFFICULTY: 2/3**

- 1 celeriac, about 1 kg/2lb 4 oz, peeled and cut into 2 cm/¾ inch cubes
- 2 tbsp olive oil, plus a drizzle
- 1 tsp black mustard seeds
- 1 tsp cumin seeds
- 3 dried red chillies, cut in half and seeds discarded (optional)
- 10 curry leaves (fresh, if available)
- 3 garlic cloves, finely diced
- 2.5 cm/1 inch piece of fresh ginger, peeled and finely diced
- 1 brown onion, diced
- 1 tsp ground turmeric
- ½ tsp chilli powder (optional)
- 1 tbsp medium curry powder
- 200 g/7 oz ripe tomatoes, chopped
- 400 ml/14 fl oz can coconut milk
- 400 g/14 oz can chickpeas, drained
- 250 g/9 oz baby spinach
- sea salt and freshly cracked black pepper

Preheat the oven to 180°C fan/200°C/400°F/gas mark 6.

Place the celeriac cubes in a large roasting tray with a drizzle of olive oil and a sprinkle of salt and pepper. Mix well, then roast in the oven for 30–40 minutes until tender, turning a couple of times during cooking.

Meanwhile, add the 2 tablespoons of olive oil to a wide-based saucepan and place over a medium-high heat. Once the oil is hot, add the mustard and cumin seeds. When the mustard seeds start to spit, add the dried red chillies (if using), curry leaves, garlic and ginger.

Let that cook for about a minute, moving continuously, then add the onion. Once the onion has softened, add the turmeric, chilli powder (if using) and curry powder. Mix well and cook for a few minutes. If it's dry, add a tablespoon or two of water.

Stir in the tomatoes, leave to simmer for a few minutes, then pour in the coconut milk. Leave the curry to simmer for about 5 minutes, then go in with the chickpeas and cooked celeriac. The curry can now simmer over a medium heat until it's a bit thicker, about 15 minutes.

Finish it off by adding the spinach, pop a lid on to allow it to wilt a bit, then mix it in.

FLANK STEAK

EF

I think this might be the recipe that illustrates the way I truly love to eat the most. A recipe that takes influences from all over the world – Chinese-inspired cumin beef, Central American tacos and Venezuelan wasakaka – all coming together in a way that balances heat, acidity and freshness, wrapped in a comforting and familiar tortilla. Build-your-own-dinners are my absolute favourite.

CUMIN BEEF TACOS WITH SALSA & WASAKAKA

SERVES: 2   **TIME: 30 MINUTES**   **DIFFICULTY: 2/3**

For the cumin beef
1 tsp cumin seeds
2 tsp Sichuan peppercorns
3 tbsp light soy sauce
1 tbsp soft brown sugar
1 tsp bicarbonate of soda
½ tsp sea salt
300 g/10½ oz flank steak, cut into thin strips
2 tbsp sunflower oil, plus extra for brushing
4 garlic cloves, finely diced
thumb-sized piece of fresh ginger, peeled and finely diced
1 brown onion, sliced
2 red peppers, deseeded and sliced
1 tsp chilli flakes
1 tbsp honey
6 small tortilla wraps or taco shells, to serve
1 tbsp olive oil

For the salsa
2 ripe tomatoes, finely diced
1 red onion, finely diced
10 g/¼ oz fresh coriander, finely chopped
juice of 1 lime
1 tbsp red wine vinegar
sea salt and freshly cracked black pepper

For the wasakaka
1 green pepper, deseeded and cut into chunks
3 spring onions, roughly chopped
1 ripe avocado, peeled, stoned and chopped into chunks
2 green chillies or fresh jalapeños
2 tbsp olive oil
juice of 1 lime
20 g/¾ oz fresh coriander, roughly chopped (plus extra to garnish)
sea salt

CONTINUED OVERLEAF

First, make the salsa. Combine all the salsa ingredients in a bowl, seasoning with salt and black pepper, then set aside.

Next, make the wasakaka. Add all the wasakaka ingredients to a blender, adding salt to taste, and blend together until just combined (it should remain a bit lumpy). Set aside.

Add the cumin seeds and Sichuan peppercorns to a pestle and mortar and grind to a coarse powder.

Add 2 tablespoons of the soy sauce, the brown sugar, bicarbonate of soda, salt and 1 teaspoon of the ground spice mix to a bowl and mix well. Add the steak strips and turn to coat all over, then leave to marinate for 10 minutes.

Heat 1 tablespoon of the sunflower oil in a large wok over a high heat, then add the marinated steak (and marinade). Fry for about 5 minutes until cooked and crispy. Alternatively, add the marinated steak (and marinade) to an air fryer, spray with oil and cook at 200°C/400°F for 10 minutes until crispy. Remove the steak to a plate and set aside.

Add the remaining tablespoon of oil to the wok and heat over a medium-high heat. Once hot, add the garlic and ginger and cook until fragrant, then add the onion, red peppers, the remaining ground spice mix and the chilli flakes and stir-fry until coloured, about 5 minutes.

Return the fried beef to the wok along with the remaining 1 tablespoon of soy sauce and the honey. Toss together and stir-fry for about 3–5 minutes.

To assemble, you can use the tortilla wraps (if using) as they are or you can make them into firm taco shells. If you would like to do this, preheat the oven to 180°C fan/200°C/400°F/gas mark 6.

Brush the tortilla wraps with some olive oil. Drape the wraps over the sides of a deep roasting or baking tray so they fold over in the middle. Roast in the oven for about 10 minutes until slightly browned – they will become firmer and hold their shape.

Fill the (soft or baked) tortilla wraps or taco shells with the fried beef mixture, top with the salsa, a dollop of the wasakaka and a little extra coriander before tucking in.

I love any dish that feels acceptable to eat at breakfast, lunch or dinner, and this Mexican-style shakshouka is just that. I'm not a big fan of large chunks of chorizo in food, but I love using it in this way where the chorizo is blended to a crumb and crisps up slightly when fried. It melts away into the dish, leaving every mouthful with that smoky sausage flavour.

MEXICAN-STYLE SHAKSHOUKA

SERVES: 3–6 **TIME: 40 MINUTES** **DIFFICULTY: 2/3**

50 g/1¾ oz chorizo, cut into chunks
2 tbsp olive oil
1 red onion, diced
3 garlic cloves, sliced
1 green pepper, deseeded and diced
2 tsp paprika
2 tsp ground cumin
1 tsp chilli flakes
1 tsp sea salt
400 g/14 oz cherry tomatoes
400 g/14 oz can black beans
6 eggs

For the pickled red onions
1 red onion, diced
juice of 1 lime
splash of olive oil
50 ml/2 fl oz apple cider vinegar

To finish and serve
6 small tortilla wraps or 200 g/7 oz loaf sourdough bread, sliced
1 ripe avocado, peeled, stoned and roughly chopped
200 g/7 oz feta cheese, broken up into rough pieces
10 g/¼ oz fresh coriander, roughly chopped
lime wedges

Throw the chorizo into a small food processor and pulse to a mince-like consistency.

Add the olive oil to a large sauté pan or Dutch oven and place over a medium-high heat. Once it's hot, add the red onion, garlic, green pepper and minced chorizo, along with the paprika, cumin, chilli flakes and salt. Cook for 5 minutes, mixing regularly.

Add the cherry tomatoes and a splash of water. Pop a lid on and cook for 10 minutes – give it a stir every now and then and make sure it isn't sticking.

Use a masher to squash the tomatoes, then add the black beans, including their juices, to the pan. Stir it all in, then leave that to bubble away over a low-medium heat for 10 minutes.

Meanwhile, make the pickled red onions by combining the red onion with the lime juice, olive oil and vinegar in a bowl. Use your hands to massage the onion and squeeze in all those juices. Set aside.

Use the back of a large spoon to create 6 small craters in the tomato sauce and crack an egg into each one. Pop a lid on the pan and cook for a few minutes until the eggs are cooked to your liking.

Meanwhile, heat the tortilla wraps according to the packet instructions or toast the sourdough and place on serving plates. Pile on the eggs and beans mixture and top with the pickled red onions, avocado, feta and coriander. Finish with the lime wedges for squeezing over.

GF, EF, V

I created this recipe in the lull between Christmas and New Year, when there's always a load of sad-looking Brussels sprouts in the supermarket that seem to know their time is up. I was adamant to make sprouts sing in a non-festive way and I think I've done just that. This recipe gives a summer lease of life to our wintry friends – it's fresh and mildly spiced, a perfect salad for any time of the year.

HOT HONEY HALLOUMI & SPROUTS

SERVES: 2–4   **TIME: 50 MINUTES**   **DIFFICULTY: 1/3**

- 200 g/7 oz Brussels sprouts, finely sliced (so they are almost shredded)
- 400 g/14 oz can chickpeas, drained and rinsed
- 1 tbsp za'atar
- pinch of sea salt
- 3 tbsp olive oil
- 450 g/1 lb halloumi, cut into cubes and drained on kitchen paper
- 2 tbsp honey
- 1 tbsp sriracha
- juice of ½ lime
- 100 g/3½ oz pomegranate seeds
- 15 g/½ oz fresh parsley, finely chopped
- 15 g/½ oz fresh coriander, finely chopped

Preheat the oven to 200°C fan/220°C/425°F/gas mark 7.

Spread the sprouts and chickpeas out over a baking tray, then sprinkle over the za'atar and a pinch of salt and drizzle over 2 tablespoons of the olive oil.

Roast in the oven for 20–30 minutes until you start getting a few crispy bits and the chickpeas have a slight crunch.

Heat the remaining 1 tablespoon of olive oil in a frying pan over a medium-high heat. When the oil is hot, add the halloumi cubes. Cook for about 6–8 minutes, turning them occasionally so there's a nice golden brown colour all over.

Meanwhile, add the honey, sriracha and lime juice to a small saucepan. Heat over a medium heat until it bubbles and becomes glossy, stirring occasionally.

Add the roasted sprouts and chickpeas, the fried halloumi, the pomegranate seeds and both herbs to a serving bowl and pour over the hot dressing. Give everything a mix so it all gets coated in the dressing, then serve.

GF, EF   *(when paired with the Chocochilli Ox Cheek Ragù)

I love finding alternative uses for any ingredient – not everything has to sit in its lane; that's the beauty of cooking and creating recipes. Celeriac seems like a daunting ingredient but it's a lot more versatile than we give it credit for. Just look at the ways it's used in this book, in a risotto here, then roasted to form an earthy curry on page 133. Celeriac's texture naturally holds well even in small pieces and it feels much lighter than a traditional risotto. Pair this with the Chocochilli Ox Cheek Ragù on pages 92–3 for a hearty meal that doesn't feel stodgy.

CELERIAC & SAFFRON RISOTTO

SERVES: 4*   **TIME: 45 MINUTES**   **DIFFICULTY: 2/3**

500 ml/18 fl oz chicken stock
pinch of saffron strands (or you can use ½ tsp ground turmeric instead – it'll give the colour but not the flavour)
200 g/7 oz smoked bacon lardons
splash of olive oil (optional)
1 shallot, finely diced
1 celeriac, about 1 kg/2 lb 4 oz, peeled and cut into small dice or brunoise (see page 202)
150 ml/5 fl oz dry white wine
40 g/1½ oz Parmesan cheese, finely grated, plus extra to serve

Add the stock to a saucepan along with the saffron (or turmeric) and heat over a low heat until hot, then keep it gently simmering.

Meanwhile, add the bacon lardons to a cold saucepan and then cook over a medium heat to render the fat and crisp up the bacon (you may need to add a splash of olive oil). This will take about 10 minutes.

Scoop the lardons out of the pan on to a plate and set aside, but leave the remaining oil in the pan as it'll be the flavour base for the rest of the dish.

Add the shallot into the bacon fat and cook over a medium heat until soft, then add the celeriac. Mix well and cook for about 5 minutes, stirring occasionally.

Turn the heat up to high and pour in the white wine. Once the wine has almost fully reduced, add the hot stock, one ladleful at a time, allowing the liquid to be absorbed by the celeriac before adding the next lot. Keep doing this until you get a lovely rich sauce, the celeriac is just cooked through and you have added all the stock.

Add half the bacon lardons back into the pan along with the grated Parmesan and mix.

Serve, topped with the remaining lardons and some extra Parmesan grated over.

GREAT
COMPANY

NEW POTATOES

EF, P (SWAP CHICKEN STOCK FOR FISH/VEG STOCK)

Korean food has a category called banchan, dedicated to side dishes that are often served to accompany a main dish or rice. Gamja Jorim is a staple of this category of food and it's a fantastic alternative use for potatoes. This is a dish that's bursting with flavour with layers upon layers of different taste profiles, a real elevation of the humble potato.

GAMJA JORIM (KOREAN BRAISED POTATO)

SERVES: 4 **TIME: 50 MINUTES** **DIFFICULTY: 1/3**

2 tbsp sunflower oil
750 g/1 lb 10 oz baby new potatoes, larger ones halved or quartered
½ brown onion, diced
2 garlic cloves, minced
2 large mild red chillies, seeds scraped out and finely diced
1 tbsp gochugaru
2 tbsp light soy sauce
1 tbsp honey
1 tbsp rice wine vinegar
1 tsp fish sauce
250 ml/9 fl oz chicken stock
sea salt

To garnish
4 spring onions, finely sliced
1 tbsp sesame seeds

Add the sunflower oil to a large pan and fry the potatoes over a medium-high heat until slightly coloured, about 5 minutes. Add a sprinkle of salt and mix.

Add the onion, garlic, chillies and gochugaru and mix well, then continue to cook for a few minutes.

While that gets lovely and fragrant, make the sauce by combining the soy sauce, honey, rice wine vinegar and fish sauce with the chicken stock. Whisk well.

Add the sauce mixture to the potatoes – you want all the potatoes just covered. Simmer, uncovered, for about 30 minutes until the sauce thickens and the potatoes are lovely and tender.

Garnish with the spring onions and sesame seeds and serve with steaming white rice.

BUTTER BEANS

GF, EF, V

Butter beans are one of my favourite storecupboard ingredients – they are super versatile, but more importantly are great at being doused in flavour. This Creole-inspired creation has all the creaminess of a standard butter bean recipe but it sings with soulful Louisiana influence that comes from the wonderful combination of dried herbs and spices.

CREAMY CREOLE BUTTER BEANS

SERVES: 2–4 AS A STARTER **TIME: 25 MINUTES** **DIFFICULTY: 1/3**

- 2 tbsp olive oil
- 1 **onion**, diced
- 4 **garlic cloves**, finely diced
- 1 tsp dried oregano
- 1 tsp dried basil
- 2 tsp paprika
- 2 x 400 g/14 oz cans butter beans
- 1 tbsp crème fraîche
- 10 g/¼ oz fresh **parsley**, roughly chopped
- sea salt

Add the olive oil to a saucepan or sauté pan over a medium heat. Once it's hot, add the onion and garlic and allow to soften and colour for a few minutes.

Season with salt, then add the oregano, basil and paprika and mix well. Cook over a medium-high heat for a few minutes until the colour darkens slightly, then stir in both cans of butter beans including their juice.

Bring to a simmer, then cook over a medium-high heat for about 10 minutes.

Once the sauce thickens a bit, stir in the crème fraîche, then sprinkle over the parsley and you're ready to serve. This is perfect with some crusty sourdough, a bowl of rice or some roasted veg.

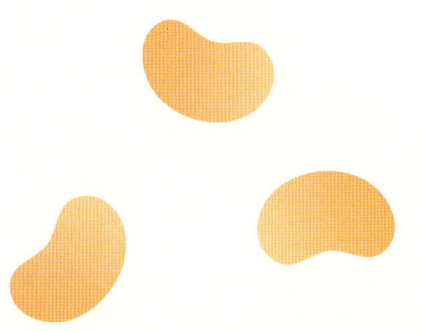

ELEVATE

GF, EF, V (no meat to accompany), Ve (no meat to accompany)

I'm that guy that buys a big 2 kg/4 lb 8 oz bag of potatoes instead of a small one because you get double the amount of potatoes for pretty much the same price. I'm also the guy that moans that my potatoes have started sprouting because I bought too many. This is a great Sunday roast dish that uses up all those extra potatoes and can be married up with whatever meat or veggie/vegan dish you like. For meat-lovers, I find a leg of lamb or whole chicken is ideal to go on top – they cook in a similar time and, while the meat rests, you can get together greens to serve alongside it.

POMMES BOULANGÈRE

SERVES: 6 **TIME: 2–3 HOURS** **DIFFICULTY: 2/3**

- 2 tbsp olive oil
- 4 onions, thinly sliced
- 8 sprigs of fresh thyme, leaves stripped off and finely chopped
- 4 sprigs of fresh rosemary, leaves stripped off and finely chopped
- 1 tbsp red wine vinegar
- 1 butternut squash, about 1 kg/ 2 lb 4 oz, peeled, deseeded and thinly sliced on a mandoline
- 1 kg/2 lb 4 oz potatoes (no need to peel as it's a rustic dish), thinly sliced on a mandoline
- about 1 litre/ 1¾ pints meat, chicken or vegetable stock (depending on what you are serving it with)
- sea salt and freshly cracked black pepper

Preheat the oven to 200°C fan/220°C/425°F/gas mark 7.

Place a large frying pan over a medium heat and add the olive oil. Once it's hot, add the onions with the thyme, rosemary and red wine vinegar and season with salt. Cook until they soften and colour slightly, mixing regularly, about 10 minutes.

Put the squash and potato slices in a large bowl and season with salt and pepper.

Layer the squash and potatoes in a baking tin or ovenproof dish, about 30 x 20 cm/12 x 8 inches. This doesn't have to be very neat, I usually do the top layer neatly and the rest less so. Every few layers, sprinkle a layer of the onion mix over. Pour over enough stock until the squash and potato slices are just covered.

If you're roasting meat on top of the potatoes (see meat options in Cook's Tips), now is the time to place it on top. For vegetarians or vegans, just cook the potato mixture on its own as is.

Place in the oven and cook for 10 minutes, then reduce the temperature to 175°C fan/195°C/385°F/gas mark 5½. If you're just cooking the potatoes without anything on top, cook for a further 1½ hours. If the meat you're cooking needs longer, the potatoes can be cooked for longer too. Once cooked, the potatoes will look nicely tinged and golden. Serve up and enjoy.

CONTINUED OVERLEAF

COOK'S TIPS →

SPICE MARINADE (FOR THE LAMB AND CHICKEN OPTIONS):

Blitz the following ingredients together to form a paste: 4 garlic cloves (peeled but left whole), 4 canned anchovy fillets, 3 tbsp olive oil, 1 tbsp apple cider vinegar, 2 tsp paprika, 1½ tsp ground cumin, 1 tsp sumac, ½ tsp ground cinnamon and 1 tsp dried mint.

MEAT OPTIONS:

Lamb

Stab holes in a leg of lamb (about 2–3 kg/4 lb 8 oz– 6 lb), big enough to fit your little finger in and about 15 of them. Cut some garlic cloves into quarters and put them in the holes along with a 2 cm/¾ inch sprig of fresh rosemary in each hole.

Brush the spice marinade (see above) all over the lamb.

Roast until the internal temperature reaches 54°C/129°F (medium-rare). Allow to rest for 15–20 minutes before carving.

Chicken

Rub the spice marinade (see above) all over the whole chicken (about 1.5 kg/3 lb) and try to work some under the skin on the breasts too.

Roast until the thigh meat reaches 72°C/162°F. Allow to rest for 15 minutes before carving.

Topside of Beef

Generously sprinkle salt and black pepper over a topside of beef (about 1.5–2 kg/3–4 lb 8 oz).

Roast until the internal temperature reaches 50°C/122°F (medium-rare). Allow to rest for 20–30 minutes before carving.

EF

I rarely write about classic recipes, but I sometimes stumble upon dishes that are staples around the world that seem to hit every note I try to hit when creating recipes. This classic side from Sichuan shows how you can combine meat and vegetables in one side dish to make it sing, something I don't think we're very good at in the western world. It's spicy and slightly smoky with a moreish numbing that builds from the Sichuan peppercorns. It goes surprisingly well with a broad range of cuisines and is a great side dish to pull out for any occasion or simply served with a bowl of steaming white rice.

SICHUAN BEANS

SERVES: 4 AS A SIDE   **TIME: 25 MINUTES**   **DIFFICULTY: 1/3**

1 tsp Sichuan peppercorns
2 tbsp sunflower oil
2 garlic cloves, grated
1 cm/½ inch piece of fresh ginger, grated
250 g/9 oz minced pork
4 dried red chillies
2 tsp sesame oil
400 g/14 oz fine green beans, trimmed
2 tbsp light soy sauce
2 tbsp oyster sauce
2 tbsp rice wine vinegar
1 tbsp honey

Add the Sichuan peppercorns to a pestle and mortar and bash a few times to create a coarse texture.

Add the sunflower oil to a wok or large pan, add the bashed peppercorns, the garlic, ginger, minced pork and dried chillies and cook over a high heat, stirring regularly, until the meat has browned and any liquid has evaporated, about 8 minutes.

Remove the pork mix from the wok/pan and set aside.

Add the sesame oil to the same wok or pan over a high heat. Add the green beans and fry until they start to char a bit on all sides (they'll also start to become a more vibrant green colour).

Add the cooked minced pork mixture back into the wok/pan and mix well.

In a small bowl or jug, make a sauce by combining the soy sauce, oyster sauce, rice wine vinegar, honey and 2 tablespoons of water. Stir thoroughly to bring it together, then pour into the wok/pan, mixing well. Place a lid on the pan for 3 minutes to allow the beans to steam through.

Remove the lid and cook over high heat for a few minutes to thicken the liquid, mixing occasionally to coat the meat and beans in the lovely sauce. Serve up and enjoy!

EF, V, Ve

*plus resting and proving

STRONG WHITE (BREAD) FLOUR

Making bread can seem pretty daunting, but focaccia is great because the outcome seems like it should take a lot more effort than it really does. Sourdough always feels like too much of a commitment, whereas focaccia isn't needy, it'll take your attention when you want it to but never demands any more. This is also a dough that can take on flavour really well and the combination of fennel seeds and curry leaves is really something else – fragrant and heady when you crunch down on the seeds and leaves, but also subtle and mellow as those flavours resonate through the bread.

FENNEL & CURRY LEAF FOCACCIA

MAKES: 1 LARGE FOCACCIA **TIME: 50 MINUTES*** **DIFFICULTY: 2/3**

- 480 ml/17 fl oz warm (tepid) water
- 7 g/⅛ oz instant yeast
- 2 tsp caster sugar
- 4–5 tbsp olive oil, plus extra for drizzling
- 575 g/1 lb 4½ oz strong white flour
- 2 tsp sea salt
- 1 tbsp fennel seeds
- 20 curry leaves (fresh, if available)

Combine the warm water, yeast, sugar and 1 tablespoon of the olive oil in a large bowl and whisk well. Leave to sit for about 5 minutes.

Add the flour and salt and mix well until it comes together to form a dough, then shape into a ball. Cover the bowl with a tea towel and set aside somewhere warm for 20 minutes.

Grab one side of the dough ball, pull it up and fold it over the rest of the dough. Repeat this a few times with different sides of the dough. Cover and rest somewhere warm for another 20 minutes. Repeat this process twice more, then cover and leave to rest for about an hour.

Heavily oil a high-sided baking tray, about 30 x 20 cm/12 x 8 inches with the remaining 3–4 tablespoons of olive oil and rub it all over. Tip the dough on to the baking tray and give it another couple of folds by pulling one side and then the other into the middle. Flip it over so the top is smooth. Cover and rest in a warm place for 2 hours.

Preheat the oven to 220°C/475°F/gas mark 9 with the fan off.

Drizzle some more olive oil on top of the dough, then use your hands and pull the dough into the corners of the tray. With your fingers slightly separated, to press into the dough to create lots of dimples all over. You'll get lovely air bubbles coming out too which is a good sign!

Sprinkle with the fennel seeds and curry leaves, then do another little round of dimpling to push them in slightly.

Bake in the oven for 20 minutes until it reaches a deep golden brown colour – you may need to turn it around halfway through if your oven heats unevenly.

Transfer to a wire rack and leave to cool, then serve warm or cold.

GF (USE GF PUFF PASTRY), EF, V　　　　　　　　　　　　　　*plus resting

I think ratatouille is actually quite boring... there, I said it! However, this recipe takes it from a quiet side dish to an elegant, attention-seeking tart that deserves all the glory. Beyond the beauty of its appearance, there's texture and lovely fresh flavours running through it. Serve this tart as a starter or even a vegetarian main with a big leafy summer salad.

SPICED RATATOUILLE TARTE TATIN

SERVES: 8　　　　**TIME: 1¾ HOURS*** 　　　　**DIFFICULTY: 2/3**

2 red peppers
6 tomatoes, 3 left whole, 3 thinly sliced
3 tbsp olive oil
1 red onion, finely diced
2 garlic cloves, grated
6 sprigs of fresh thyme
1 tsp granulated sugar

a few knobs (about 30 g/1 oz) of salted butter
1 courgette, thinly sliced on a mandoline
2 aubergines, thinly sliced on a mandoline
320 g/11¼ oz ready-rolled puff pastry sheet

Preheat the oven to 180°C fan/200°C/400°F/gas mark 6.

Char the 2 red peppers and the 3 whole tomatoes – either use a blowtorch or gas hob to do this, or pop them under a hot grill.

Once charred all over, place in a heatproof bowl and cover with clingfilm to steam and loosen the skin for about 15 minutes.

Add 2 tablespoons of the olive oil to a saucepan over a medium-high heat. Add the red onion and garlic along with 3 sprigs of thyme and cook for 5 minutes until slightly coloured and softened.

Meanwhile, use a butter knife to scrape the charred skin off the peppers and tomatoes, deseed the peppers and roughly chop them all into chunks.

CONTINUED OVERLEAF

Add them to the saucepan and mix well. Cover and cook over a medium heat for about 10–15 minutes, then remove from the heat and either blend to a sauce using a stick blender in the pan, or, if using a closed worktop blender, wait for the mix to cool down before blending.

Add the remaining 1 tablespoon of olive oil to an ovenproof frying pan (about 25 cm/10 inches in diameter), sprinkle the granulated sugar over the oil, add the butter and throw in the remaining 3 sprigs of thyme.

Arrange the courgette, aubergine and tomato slices in an overlapping spiral in the pan.

Cook, without stirring, over a medium heat for about 5 minutes to allow the sugar to slightly caramelize.

Pour the red pepper and tomato sauce evenly over the spiral. Unroll the puff pastry sheet, then place it over the pan. Cut it to size, leaving a slight border all around the edge, then gently press the pastry down, tucking the edges down inside the pan.

Use a knife to poke holes into the pastry to allow steam to be released – this is an important step to prevent moisture building up. Make sure the holes go through the full thickness of the pastry.

Bake in the oven for 40–50 minutes until the pastry is risen and golden brown in colour.

Remove from the oven and leave the tarte to rest for about 15 minutes. Place a board or plate on top and flip it over, inverting the tarte – do it carefully but with purpose! Slice and plate up!

GF, EF, V

I'm sure most things taste good on a honeymoon but these lentils really took me by surprise on my mine. They were added to the order simply to address my constant worry that there's not going to be enough food, but as soon as they arrived they stole the show. Deep and peppery with a hint of Scotch bonnet fire – these incredible lentils were made by this one lady, CiCi, out of a tiny little shack on a small section of beach covered by beautiful swooping palm trees with crystal clear waters coming right up to you. All of that was ignored as soon as those lentils hit my palate. I couldn't get enough, shovelling them in until not one pulse was left.

HONEYMOON LENTILS

SERVES: 4 **TIME: 40 MINUTES** **DIFFICULTY: 1/3**

1 tbsp olive oil
1 brown onion, diced
4 garlic cloves, finely diced
1 cm/½ inch piece of fresh ginger, peeled and finely diced
8 sprigs of fresh thyme, leaves stripped off
2 tbsp Jamaican curry powder
½ tbsp tomato purée
2 x 400 g/14 oz cans green lentils
1 Scotch bonnet
sea salt and freshly cracked black pepper

To finish
drizzle of double cream
juice of ½ lime
15 g/½ oz fresh coriander, chopped

Add the olive oil to a saucepan over a medium-high heat. Once it's hot, add the onion and cook till soft and coloured, about 10 minutes, then add the garlic, ginger and thyme and cook for 2 minutes.

Season with salt and a generous amount of cracked black pepper. Stir in the Jamaican curry powder and allow to cook for a few minutes – the curry powder will turn a darker colour.

Add the tomato purée, both cans of lentils (liquid and all) and the whole Scotch bonnet. If you put the Scotch bonnet in whole, it won't make the dish spicy, it'll just add flavour.

Cover with 400 ml/14 fl oz of water and bring to a simmer, then cook for 20 minutes, uncovered.

Finish with a drizzle of double cream and the lime juice, then sprinkle with the coriander and serve.

GF, EF, P

Arroz de Tomate is a Portuguese family staple made simply with their beautiful ripe tomatoes and rice. It's a great accompaniment for fish, meat and vegetables and often sits quietly as an ever-present companion. This recipe, however, livens things up a bit and takes this faithful, quiet side and makes it sing. The addition of anchovies to the base provides a seafood saltiness that ends up running throughout the dish, and the chilli flakes give that little bit of heat to bring some warm excitement to the table.

ARROZ DE TOMATE

SERVES: 4–6 **TIME: 50–60 MINUTES** **DIFFICULTY: 2/3**

- 300 g/10½ oz baby plum tomatoes
- 1 tbsp olive oil, plus extra for drizzling
- 4 canned anchovy fillets
- 4 garlic cloves, finely diced
- 1 brown onion, finely diced
- 1 red pepper, deseeded and finely diced
- 1 tsp chilli flakes
- 250 ml/9 fl oz dry white wine
- 400 g/14 oz ripe tomatoes, roughly chopped (or use 400 g/14 oz can good-quality chopped tomatoes)
- 400 g/14 oz basmati rice, washed and drained
- small handful of fresh parsley, chopped
- juice of 1 lemon
- sea salt

Preheat the oven to 200°C fan/220°C/425°F/gas mark 7.

Place the baby plum tomatoes in a roasting tray, drizzle with olive oil and sprinkle with salt, then roast in the oven until they start to blister, about 20 minutes.

Add the 1 tablespoon of olive oil to a large sauté pan over a medium-high heat. Once it's hot, add the anchovy fillets and garlic and cook until the anchovies start breaking down and the garlic just starts to colour.

Add the onion, red pepper and chilli flakes to the pan and season with salt.

Add the white wine and cook over a high heat until it is reduced completely.

Add the chopped ripe (or canned) tomatoes to the pan along with the roasted baby plum tomatoes (reserve a few for garnishing, keep in the oven with the oven off to retain their heat). Mix everything together well, then stir in the washed rice. Cook over a medium heat, allowing the rice to absorb the flavours for a few minutes.

Add 800 ml/28 fl oz of water to the pan and cover with a lid. Bring to the boil, then reduce the heat to low and cook for 15–20 minutes or until the rice is cooked through and the liquid has gone.

To serve, sprinkle with the parsley, the reserved roasted baby plum tomatoes and a good squeeze of lemon juice.

EF, V, Ve

I often look at cauliflower like the chicken of the vegetable world – it doesn't bring a huge amount to the table on its own but is a fantastic vessel for flavour and smoke. That's probably why these jerk cauliflower wedges work just as well as jerk chicken does. Cauliflower is also the best example of how a bit of char can take a mundane veg to something with complexity and depth. Add in a fiery and herby jerk marinade and you're on to a winner.

JERK CAULIFLOWER WEDGES

SERVES: 4 AS A SIDE   **TIME: 1 HOUR**   **DIFFICULTY: 2/3**

1 cauliflower, leaves intact
1 red onion, quartered
3 spring onions, roughly chopped
1 Scotch bonnet
2 tbsp soft brown sugar
2 tbsp light soy sauce
1 tbsp apple cider vinegar
juice of 1 lemon
4 sprigs of fresh thyme
1 bay leaf
4 pimento seeds (allspice berries)
1 tsp sea salt, plus extra for the cauli water
½ tsp ground cinnamon
olive oil, for drizzling

Preheat the oven to 180°C fan/200°C/400°F/gas mark 6.

Blanch the whole cauliflower in a pan of salted boiling water for about 5 minutes – don't let the water boil heavily, just steaming is about right. Remove and set aside to drain and steam-dry.

Make the jerk marinade by blending together the red onion, spring onions, Scotch bonnet, brown sugar, soy sauce, apple cider vinegar, lemon juice, thyme (stalks and all), bay leaf, pimento seeds, measured salt and cinnamon. Blend for at least 3 minutes to make sure everything has incorporated well into a paste.

Cut the cauliflower into wedges (eighths) and place in a roasting tray (ideally on a rack). Brush some of the jerk marinade all over the sides and top of each cauli wedge and drizzle with olive oil.

Roast in the oven for 20 minutes. Remove from the oven, then flip each cauli wedge and brush the remaining jerk marinade on the other side. Drizzle with a bit more olive oil and return to the oven for another 20–30 minutes. You're aiming for a slight char on some edges of the cauliflower.

Serve as part of a crowd-pleasing spread as a side dish, or alongside some roasted meats.

GF, EF

Having made this for dinner parties on a number of occasions, I can vouch for it being a true crowd-pleaser. All the work happens at the start and the flavour begins to develop from the crust on the short ribs to all the beautiful aromatics that bring out the Malaysian essence. A hearty and decadent showstopper.

MALAYSIAN BEEF SHORT RIBS

SERVES: 4 **TIME: 3 HOURS 40 MINUTES** **DIFFICULTY: 2/3**

- 1.2–1.6 kg/2 lb 10 oz–3 lb 8 oz individual beef short ribs
- 1 large onion, cut into chunks
- 6 garlic cloves, peeled but left whole
- large thumb-sized piece of fresh ginger, peeled
- large thumb-sized piece of fresh galangal (or use 1 tbsp galangal paste)
- 2 sticks of lemongrass, 1 sliced into small pieces, the other left whole
- 3 red chillies, stems removed
- 2 tbsp coconut oil or sunflower oil
- 80 g/3 oz desiccated coconut
- 350 ml/12 fl oz red wine
- 1 cinnamon stick
- 4 fresh makrut lime leaves
- 500 ml/18 fl oz beef stock
- 400 ml/18 fl oz coconut milk
- sea salt and freshly cracked black pepper

Get your short ribs out of the refrigerator 30 minutes before you start cooking – this is a good habit to get into when cooking (most) meats. Season them well with salt and black pepper all over.

Preheat the oven to 140°C fan/160°C/300°F/gas mark 3.

Add the onion, garlic, ginger, galangal, sliced lemongrass stick and red chillies to a food processor and blitz until you form a paste. Set aside.

Add the coconut oil or sunflower oil to a large casserole dish over a high heat. Once it starts to smoke, add the short ribs and sear each side until you get a lovely dark brown crust all over. You may have to do this in batches. Remove the ribs from the pan once they are seared. Set aside.

Turn the heat down to medium and add the blitzed onion paste. Fry this until the colour starts to darken slightly, about 5 minutes. You'll need to mix it quite regularly and make sure you scrape up all the lovely beef flavour that's stuck to the bottom of the pan.

Meanwhile, place a frying pan over a medium heat and add the desiccated coconut. Cook for about 4 minutes until it turns a golden brown colour – keep stirring to prevent it burning. Set aside once it's done.

Add the red wine to the onion mix in the casserole dish and cook over a medium-high heat until the wine is reduced by half.

Bash the remaining lemongrass stick and add it to the casserole along with the cinnamon stick and lime leaves. Stir in the beef stock, coconut milk and the toasted desiccated coconut.

Return the beef short ribs to the casserole, place a lid or cartouche on top (see page 214), then transfer to the oven and cook for 3 hours until the beef is meltingly tender.

This goes perfectly with some steamed white rice, or if you prefer noodles, you can add some dried noodles straight to the liquid in the casserole to rehydrate them and you'll be left with a lovely noodle dish with tender, melt-in-the-mouth beef short ribs.

EF, V, Ve   *2 as a main

Aubergines are incredibly versatile in the flavours they can take on, the cuisines they pop up in and the methods you can use to cook them. Steaming aubergines is probably one of the healthier cooking processes but it's also a great way to bring out their soft fleshy texture. I've cut these into 'fingers' to give them structure while still being soft. This dish is great as part of a big spread, as everyone can cut off a couple of fingers each, or you can serve it simply with some steamed rice.

STEAMED STICKY AUBERGINE

SERVES: 2   **TIME: 50 MINUTES**   **DIFFICULTY: 2/3**

2 aubergines
2 tbsp olive oil
1 red onion, finely diced
3 garlic cloves, grated or finely diced
2.5 cm/1 inch piece of fresh ginger, peeled and grated or finely diced
1–2 tsp chilli flakes (depending on heat preference)
10 curry leaves (fresh, if available)
2 tbsp light soy sauce
2 tbsp rice wine vinegar
2 tbsp light brown sugar
1 tbsp tomato purée
2 tsp cornflour
juice of 1 lime
sea salt

To garnish
chopped fresh coriander leaves
chopped spring onions

Use a sharp knife to make one long cut down each aubergine from just below the green calyx down to the bottom, about 5 mm/¼ inch deep. Place both in a steamer and steam for 20 minutes (see Cook's Tip).

Once steamed, set the aubergines aside to cool until handleable. Place on a chopping board, then extend the original long cut so it goes all the way through each aubergine but not through the calyx. Rotate 90 degrees and make another cut from just below the calyx through to the other side, right down through the length of the aubergine. At this point you'll be left with 4 long quarters attached at the top. Do this another two times so you're left with 8 long strips or 'fingers'.

Place a large frying pan or sauté pan over a medium-high heat with 1 tablespoon of olive oil. Once hot, place each aubergine down flat in the pan with the 8 'fingers' spread out. Season with salt. Turn the aubergines after 2 minutes.

Remove the aubergines and set aside again. Add the remaining tablespoon of olive oil to the pan and add the red onion, garlic, ginger, chilli flakes and curry leaves. Cook over a medium-high heat until fragrant and the onion starts to soften. Add the soy sauce, rice wine vinegar, brown sugar and tomato purée to the pan, mix well, then add 400 ml/14 fl oz of water. Bring to a simmer for about 5 minutes.

Mix the cornflour with 2 tablespoons of water in a small bowl to form a slurry, then stir into the pan. Add the aubergines back in, then leave to bubble for 5 minutes so the sauce thickens and is glossy. Finish with a squeeze of lime.

Garnish with a sprinkling of chopped coriander and spring onions and serve on steaming rice.

COOK'S TIP → If you don't have a steamer, it's very easy to make your own: get a large pan and place a small heatproof bowl in it upside down. Place the aubergines on a small shallow heatproof tray and place this on top of the upturned bowl. Fill the pan with boiling water so it comes up to about 1–2 cm/½–¾ inch below the aubergine tray. Place a lid on the pan and steam over a medium-high heat as above.

P

I think these are the ultimate snack – crispy and fishy with a sharp and spicy sauce, and everything I look for in a moreish mouthful. I first made tempura mussels in an invention test on MasterChef and they went down an absolute treat, with the judges requesting a bucketload of them, which made me realize just how great a snack they would be. We don't generally associate mussels with much texture other than soft and slightly chewy, but the simple tempura batter in this recipe cocoons the delish mussels in a light and crispy cage that adds a whole new dimension of joy to eating them.

TEMPURA MUSSELS WITH SPICY TARTARE

SERVES: 6 AS A SNACK **TIME: 45 MINUTES** **DIFFICULTY: 3/3**

For the mussels
1 kg/2 lb 4 oz mussels in shell
1 tbsp olive oil
1 brown onion, diced
4 garlic cloves, finely diced
1 tsp cayenne pepper
250 ml/9 fl oz dry white wine
sunflower oil, for deep-frying
lemon wedge, to serve
sea salt

For the spicy tartare sauce
4 tbsp mayonnaise
juice of ½ lemon
1 large gherkin or 4 cornichons, drained and finely diced
2 tbsp capers, drained and finely chopped
½ shallot, finely diced
15 g/½ oz fresh parsley, finely chopped

For the tempura batter
75 ml/2½ fl oz soda water
40 g/1½ oz plain flour
20 g/¾ oz cornflour
2 ice cubes (optional)

CONTINUED OVERLEAF

Prep the mussels according to the instructions on page 212.

Add the olive oil to a large saucepan with a lid, then when it's hot, add the onion and garlic and cook over a medium-high heat. Once the onion softens a bit and the garlic is fragrant, add the cayenne pepper and season with salt. Mix well, then add the white wine and allow it to reduce almost completely.

Drain the mussels and add to the pan, give it a quick mix, then pop the lid on. Cook for 4–5 minutes until the mussels have opened (discard any that are still closed).

Strain the contents of the pan through a sieve, reserving the mussels and liquid separately. Add the liquid to a clean saucepan and cook over a medium-high heat until it reduces to about 2 tablespoons.

While that reduces, remove the mussels from their shells and place on kitchen paper to dry. Discard the shells.

To make the spicy tartare sauce, add the mayonnaise to a bowl along with the reduced mussel liquid and the lemon juice and mix well. Add the gherkin or cornichons, capers, shallot and parsley to the mayo mix and mix well. Set aside.

Heat enough sunflower oil in a deep-fat fryer (if you have one) or in a heavy-based saucepan (don't fill the pan more than two-thirds full) to 180°C/350°F (or until a small piece of bread browns in 30 seconds).

While the oil is heating, prepare the tempura batter. Add the soda water, flour and cornflour to a bowl and gently mix together with chopsticks or the back of a wooden spoon. You don't want to overwork this as you want to reduce any gluten development. Adding the ice cubes can help to keep the mixture cool and improve crispiness.

Once the oil is hot, add the mussels to the batter to coat and then add to the hot oil in batches. Be wary as they are prone to spitting. It'll take about 1 minute to cook each batch and they will look crispy and golden brown when ready. Remove them with a slotted spoon and drain on kitchen paper, while you deep-fry the rest.

Serve up the crispy tempura mussels with an extra squeeze of lemon and the spicy tartare sauce.

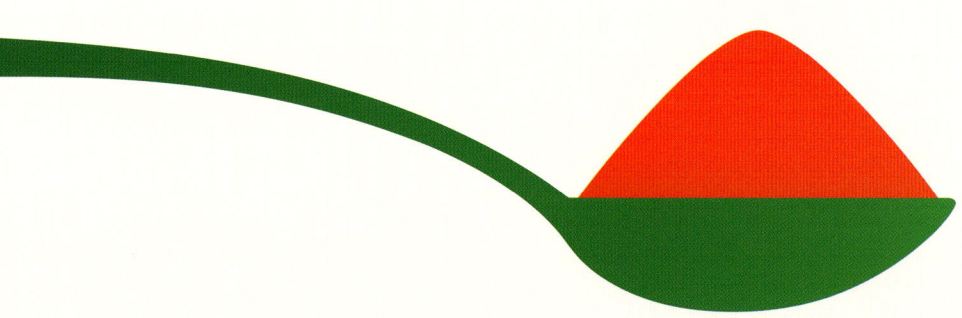

GF, EF   *as part of a spread

As soon as we'd see my dad prepping these chops, it was clear that we were either hosting a barbecue or off to someone else's – they were always on the menu. These are the epitome of rustic flavour building – my dad eyeballs every ingredient and understands whether it needs a bit of this or a bit of that simply from the colour, smell or feel. The chops are made for barbecue smokiness and really benefit from having little crunchy corners of char. Mutton can be tough and chewy, but the two-step cooking process in this recipe gives them that bit of tenderness we're always looking for. Pair these with the Kothu Panzanella on page 116 for my ultimate Tamil Sri Lankan summer meal.

APPA'S BARBECUE MUTTON CHOPS

SERVES: 5–10*   **TIME: 50 MINUTES**   **DIFFICULTY: 1/3**

- **10 mutton back chops**, fat removed
- **2 red onions**, diced
- **3 tomatoes**, diced
- **5 garlic cloves**, cut into quarters lengthways (see Cook's Tip)
- **2.5 cm/1 inch piece of fresh ginger**, peeled and finely diced
- **10–15 curry leaves** (fresh, if available)
- **3 green chillies** (optional)
- **1–2 tbsp Sri Lankan roasted curry powder** (depending on spice preference)
- **4 tbsp Greek-style yogurt**
- **sea salt**

Preheat the oven to 180°C fan/200°C/400°F/gas mark 6.

Add the chops, red onions, tomatoes, garlic, ginger, curry leaves, whole green chillies (if using), curry powder and Greek-style yogurt to a roasting tray, season with salt and mix well with your hands – this must be done with your hands for the best results.

Cover with foil and roast in the oven for 30 minutes, giving it a stir and removing the foil after 15 minutes.

Finish the chops off on a hot barbecue or in an air fryer at 200°C/400°F for 5 minutes on each side. You can also place them under a hot grill, if you prefer. While the chops finish cooking, keep the tray of roasted veg and aromatics in a warm oven. The mutton can go back in this tray once cooked and served with all the flavours in the tray.

COOK'S TIP → Why cut the garlic cloves into quarters lengthways, you ask? I don't know, that's just how my dad does it so it must be right! You can always substitute them with some grated garlic but the lengthways garlic quarters really are a must, they add texture and add a slight caramelized garlic flavour when cooked.

HISPI CABBAGE

GF, EF, V, Ve

This was a real staple in our household growing up, one of my parents' ways of getting greens into me and a dish that I didn't fully appreciate until I was older. Some dishes don't need to be the star of the show but their presence is vital to make the centrepiece sing and that is exactly what this does. A Tamil chicken curry is good, but it's great when it's eaten alongside this, and that's another way of showing how a basic ingredient like hispi cabbage can elevate an entire meal. Boring hispi cabbage suddenly becomes exciting and vibrant when it's paired with these wonderful spices that are so familiar from the food of my childhood.

GOVA VARAI

SERVES: 4 **TIME: 30 MINUTES** **DIFFICULTY: 1/3**

- 1 hispi cabbage, finely sliced into 5 mm/¼ inch slices
- 40 g/1½ oz desiccated coconut
- 60 ml/2¼ oz boiling water
- 1 tsp ground turmeric
- 2 tsp sea salt, plus extra to season
- 1 tbsp sunflower oil
- ½ tsp black mustard seeds
- ½ tsp fennel seeds
- 10–15 curry leaves (fresh, if available)
- 2–4 dried red chillies, cut into quarters and deseeded (depending on spice preference)
- 1 red onion, sliced
- 1 tbsp channa dhal

Add the cabbage to a large bowl.

In a small bowl, combine the desiccated coconut and boiling water. Mix well, then add this to the cabbage along with the turmeric and salt. Get your hands in and mix this all together, squeezing as you mix to make sure everything joins the party. Set aside.

Heat a wok over a high heat and add the sunflower oil. Once it's hot, add the mustard and fennel seeds. When the mustard seeds start to spit, add the curry leaves, dried red chilli quarters, red onion and channa dhal. Mix well.

Cook and stir until the onion starts to soften and colour, then add the hispi cabbage mixture. Cook for about 10 minutes, mixing it around every minute or two. Season to taste with extra salt, if needed, then serve with your favourite curries and rice or flatbreads.

P

I love a cheap alternative to a fancy dish and this brioche fish roll gives all the decadence of a lobster roll but with accessible salmon instead. Small tips like toasting the outside of the brioche roll before assembling make a huge difference to both texture and flavour. This makes for a delicious weekend lunch or a lazy dinner that feels casually decadent.

BRIOCHE FISH ROLLS

SERVES: 2   **TIME: 20 MINUTES**   **DIFFICULTY: 1/3**

1 tbsp olive oil
1 shallot or small onion, finely diced
1 garlic clove, thinly sliced
2 skinless salmon fillets, cut into cubes
1½ tbsp mayonnaise
1 tsp Dijon mustard
juice of ¼ lemon, plus the remaining lemon cut into wedges to finish
½ tsp cayenne pepper
1 large gherkin, drained and roughly chopped
1 tbsp capers, drained and roughly chopped
small handful of fresh dill, chopped
2 brioche buns, cut in half
sea salt

Add the olive oil to a frying pan, then add the shallot or onion and garlic and cook over a medium-high heat until a bit coloured. Add the salmon cubes and cook for about 5 minutes, turning regularly to get colour on all sides (see Cook's Tip). Season with a sprinkle of salt.

Remove the pan from the heat and set aside to cool.

In a bowl, combine the mayo, mustard, lemon juice, cayenne pepper, gherkin, capers and chopped dill (reserving some for the topping). Mix well.

Add the cooked salmon along with the shallot/onion and garlic and mix well, being careful not to break up the salmon.

Toast the halved brioche buns by placing them in the empty salmon pan over a medium heat until dark golden on each side.

Fill the rolls with the salmon mixture. Finish with a squeeze of the lemon wedges and the reserved dill. Tuck in and enjoy!

COOK'S TIP → You can cook the salmon in an air fryer, if you prefer. Simply place the salmon cubes in an air fryer and cook at 200°C/400°F for 10 minutes, turning halfway through. Fry the shallot/onion and garlic in a pan as above until lightly coloured and softened, then combine with the air-fried salmon cubes and continue as above.

SWEEET TREATS

CREAM CHEESE

V

*plus infusing, cooling and chilling

Miso paste has been added to desserts for years now. It brings a deep savoury note to something super sweet and creates the effect of salted caramel or salted chocolate. However, infusing the miso into the cream in this recipe means that every bite benefits from this collision of savoury sweetness. The most important bit of advice for this dessert is that you should see a concerning wobble when you remove the cheesecake from the oven. That's the key to getting a silky smooth cheese layer.

MISO BURNT BASQUE CHEESECAKE

SERVES: 8 **TIME: 1 HOUR*** **DIFFICULTY: 2/3**

450 ml/16 fl oz double cream
75 g/2¾ oz white miso paste
825 g/1 lb 13 oz cream cheese
300 g/10½ oz caster sugar
5 large eggs
40 g/1½ oz plain flour

Add the double cream and miso paste to a saucepan and heat gently. Mix gently until the miso is dissolved, then remove from the heat and leave to infuse for about 15 minutes.

Strain the cream to remove any bits and then chill the mixture in the refrigerator for 1 hour.

Preheat the oven to 200°C fan/220°C/425°F/gas mark 7. Double-line a 21 cm/8 inch round, deep, springform cake tin with greaseproof paper.

Beat the cream cheese and sugar together in a mixing bowl or stand mixer until combined. Add the chilled miso-infused cream and mix again. Add the eggs, one by one, while mixing continuously. Sift in the flour and then give it one final mix to combine.

Pour the mixture into the prepped cake tin and level the surface.

Pop into the oven and bake for about 40 minutes. It's ready when it still wobbles when you shake it and the top is a bit burnt.

Remove from the oven and leave to cool (in the tin) on a wire rack. Once cool, refrigerate for 6–8 hours (ideally overnight) before serving.

To serve, carefully remove the cheesecake from the tin, then cut into slices and tuck in!

V

I have an incredibly sweet tooth, like seriously, insanely sweet, so as you can imagine, me and banoffee pie have a great relationship. But, as with all relationships, it's important to test the limits and see just how far you can push it. I think this dessert, just about, reaches the limits of my sweetness. A standard banoffee pie has a layer of sliced bananas and some whipped cream to ease the sweetness of the base and caramel, but this elevated version gives no relief. Caramelized bananas replace fresh ones and a thick layer of Italian meringue replaces the cream. Bring out your blowtorch to add a bit of drama just before you serve it. You're gonna love this dessert, it's almost ecstatic, but I think it should also come with a warning. This is your warning.

BANOFFEE MERINGUE PIE

SERVES: 8 **TIME: 50 MINUTES** **DIFFICULTY: 3/3**

400 g/14 oz digestive biscuits
295 g/10½ oz butter
75 g/2¾ oz soft brown sugar, plus an extra sprinkle
400 g/14 oz can condensed milk
3 bananas, peeled and cut in half lengthways
200 g/7 oz caster sugar
4 large egg whites (consider using the yolks for the Udon Gochu Carbonara on page 81)

Add the biscuits to a food processor and blitz, or place in a freezer bag and pound with a rolling pin, to make fine crumbs. Tip into a bowl.

Melt 200 g/7 oz of the butter in a saucepan over a medium heat, allowing it to brown for nuttiness.

Add the melted butter to the biscuit crumbs and mix well. Tip into a 21 cm/8½ inch round springform tin or loose-based tart tin. Use the bottom of a glass to press the mixture evenly across the base and sides to create a case. Refrigerate while you make the caramel.

Melt 75 g/2¾ oz of the remaining butter in a saucepan over a low heat, then stir in the measured brown sugar. Add the condensed milk and cook over a medium heat while stirring until it darkens, about 3–5 minutes. Pour into the biscuit base and level out.

Add the remaining 20 g/¾ oz of butter to a frying pan along with the sprinkle of brown sugar and place over a medium heat. Place the bananas, cut-side down, into the pan and cook until caramelized, about 2–3 minutes. Layer the bananas on to the caramel, then refrigerate while you make the meringue.

For the meringue, add the caster sugar and 50 ml/2 fl oz of water to a saucepan, stir over a medium heat until the sugar has dissolved, then heat, without stirring, to 118°C/244°F.

Whisk the egg whites in the bowl of a stand mixer till frothy, then gradually whisk in the hot sugar syrup in a thin, steady stream. Once all the sugar syrup is added, turn up the speed of the mixer to full. Keep whisking until the meringue is stiff and shiny and the temperature of the bowl has decreased enough to hold.

Dollop the meringue on to the pie and create wisps, then char with a blowtorch and serve.

V *plus cooling and optional freezing

This recipe is just pure indulgence. There are savoury notes running through this entire dessert from the addition of miso to both the churros and dipping sauce. It's undeniably naughty but oh so irresistible. You'll find the majority of these ingredients in your pantry, perfect for those rainy days where you've got nothing to do but cook and eat tasty treats.

MISO CHURROS WITH CHOCOLATE MISO DIPPING SAUCE

SERVES: 4 **TIME: 45 MINUTES*** **DIFFICULTY: 2/3**

For the churros
- 70 g/2½ oz unsalted butter
- 2 tbsp red miso paste
- 2 tbsp caster sugar
- 180 g/6¼ oz plain flour
- 2 eggs
- sunflower or vegetable oil, for deep-frying (optional)

For the cinnamon sugar
- 4 tbsp caster sugar
- 2 tsp ground cinnamon

For the chocolate dipping sauce
- 200 ml/7 fl oz double cream
- 1 tbsp red miso paste
- 100 g/3½ oz plain chocolate, broken into pieces

Make the churros. Add the butter, miso paste and caster sugar to a pan, along with 300 ml/10 fl oz of water, place over a medium-high heat and bring to the boil, stirring occasionally.

Once it's boiled and everything has dissolved, add the flour and mix continuously for a few minutes until the dough is smooth and comes away from the sides of the pan easily. Transfer the dough to a heatproof bowl and allow to cool for 5–10 minutes.

Add an egg to the dough and mix until fully incorporated, then add the remaining egg and repeat. Transfer the mixture to a piping bag fitted with a star nozzle.

Line a baking tray with greaseproof paper. Pipe the dough into strips (each about 10 cm/4 inches long) on the greaseproof paper.

Freeze for 20 minutes if you plan to air-fry these. If you're deep-frying them, cut the paper so each churro is on its own small rectangle.

Heat enough sunflower or vegetable oil in a deep-fat fryer (if you have one) or in a heavy-based saucepan (don't fill the pan more than two-thirds full) to 180°C/350°F (or until a small piece of bread browns in 30 seconds).

Drop each churro on its paper into the hot oil – the paper will come off on its own and can be picked out. Deep-fry in batches until deep golden brown, about 2–3 minutes. Using a slotted spoon or spider strainer, remove the cooked churros (and the paper – discard this) to some kitchen paper to absorb the excess oil, while you cook the rest in the same way.

CONTINUED OVERLEAF

If air-frying, place the slightly frozen churros on to an air fryer tray and spray with oil, then cook in the air fryer at 200°C/400°F for 15 minutes, turning occasionally.

Meanwhile, for the cinnamon sugar, combine the caster sugar and cinnamon in a tray or bowl. Set aside.

To make the dipping sauce, heat the double cream and miso paste in a saucepan over a medium-high heat, stirring constantly, until the miso has dissolved. Heat until just steaming and then pour this over the plain chocolate in a heatproof jug. Leave to sit for 2 minutes, then blend with a stick blender to make a smooth sauce.

Once the churros are all cooked, roll them in the cinnamon sugar to coat. Serve them warm with the chocolate sauce and get dipping!

V

There's not a lot wrong with a classic STP. In fact, pretty much everything is right about it, but that doesn't stop me from figuring out a few ways to push it a little bit further. The slight gingery heat that lingers throughout this dessert is super warming and makes everything that little bit more festive. Also, why just soak dates in water when you can soak them in the slightly spiced caramel flavours of Coca-Cola?!

GINGER & COLA STICKY TOFFEE PUDDING

SERVES: 6–8 **TIME: 1 HOUR** **DIFFICULTY: 2/3**

For the sticky toffee pudding
200 g/7 oz stoned dates
1 tsp bicarbonate of soda
200 ml/7 fl oz Coca-Cola
80 g/3 oz unsalted **butter,** at room temperature, plus extra for greasing
100 g/3½ oz soft brown sugar
1 tsp ground ginger
2 eggs
2 tbsp black treacle
160 g/5¾ oz plain flour
2 tsp baking powder

For the sauce
130 ml/4¼ fl oz Coca-Cola
240 g/8½ oz soft brown sugar
1 tsp ground ginger
2 tsp black treacle
120 g/4 oz unsalted **butter,** at room temperature
200 ml/7 fl oz double cream

ice cream, to serve

Preheat the oven to 170°C fan/190°C/375°F/gas mark 5. Grease six 180 ml/6 fl oz dariole moulds or a 25 x 18 cm/10 x 7 inch baking tin with butter.

Make the pudding. Add the dates to a small saucepan with the bicarbonate of soda and Coca-Cola. Bring to the boil, then remove from the heat and set aside.

In a mixing bowl, beat together the butter and brown sugar until light and fluffy, then add the ground ginger. Whisk again, then add the eggs, one at a time, whisking between and ensuring the first is fully incorporated before adding the second.

Add the treacle to the mixture and mix again. Sift in the flour and baking powder, then fold them in. Mash the soaked dates and add them to the batter along with all the juices in the saucepan and give everything one last mix.

CONTINUED OVERLEAF

Divide the batter between the prepped dariole moulds or baking tin (spreading it evenly if using the baking tin). Bake in the oven for 25–30 minutes if using dariole moulds or 35–40 minutes with a baking tin until a skewer comes out clean.

Meanwhile, make the toffee sauce. Add the cola to a small saucepan over a high heat. Reduce to about a third of its volume, then reduce to a medium heat and add the sugar, ginger, treacle and butter. Whisk until everything is incorporated, then turn off the heat and add the cream. Whisk and set aside.

Once the puddings are done, remove from the oven and pour a layer of the toffee sauce over the top if using one baking tin, or tip them out of their individual moulds into serving bowls and lather on a decent amount of sauce. Serve any extra sauce alongside. Top each serving with a dollop of vanilla ice cream.

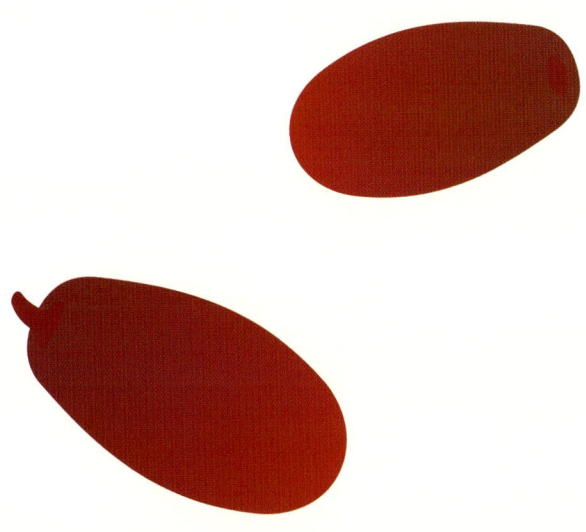

POLENTA

GF, V

Polenta is a great ingredient to use – it's cheap, accessible and goes a long way, not to mention being a great option for creating luxurious gluten-free desserts. It adds a lovely texture to cakes while still being light and airy. Compared to most of my sweet recipes, this cake feels quite sophisticated and something you'd be happy to serve to your in-laws. It's sweet but also slightly sour and is finished perfectly with some crème fraîche and lemon zest.

PLUM POLENTA CAKE

SERVES: 6–8 **TIME: 1 HOUR** **DIFFICULTY: 1/3**

For the cake
- 175 g/6 oz caster sugar
- 3 eggs
- 175 ml/6 fl oz olive oil, plus extra for greasing
- 1 tbsp natural yogurt
- juice of 2 lemons
- 200 g/7 oz ground almonds
- 80 g/3 oz fine polenta
- 1 tsp baking powder
- 4 ripe plums, stoned and each cut into 6 wedges

For the syrup
- juice of 1 lemon
- 3 tbsp honey

To finish and serve
- finely grated zest of 1 lemon
- crème fraîche

Preheat the oven to 175°C fan/195°C/385°F/gas mark 5½. Grease a 30 cm/12 inch oval ovenproof dish with olive oil. Greasing with olive oil adds a lovely, subtle savoury note to the base and sides of this cake.

Whisk the sugar and eggs together in a bowl until light and fluffy. Add the olive oil, yogurt and lemon juice and whisk until combined.

Add the ground almonds, polenta and baking powder and whisk together well.

Pour the cake batter into the prepped dish and spread evenly. Arrange the plum wedges on top of the batter.

Bake in the oven for 35 minutes, until risen and golden brown and a skewer inserted into the middle comes out clean.

Meanwhile, for the syrup, combine the lemon juice and honey in a small saucepan over a medium heat and cook until well combined, about 2 minutes.

Remove the cake from the oven when it's ready, then poke holes into the top and pour over the honey and lemon syrup. Leave it to soak in for a few minutes, then sprinkle with the lemon zest and serve with crème fraîche.

V

*plus cooling

It's fair to say I've just taken two of my big culinary loves and combined them to create this recipe. Anna and I head to Portugal fairly regularly and my Pastel de Nata count is usually embarrassingly high by the second afternoon. It's not rare to find me sneaking off for secret PDNs while we're out and about, or taking myself off to breakfast before anyone else so I can sneak in a couple without judgement. Naturally, I'm also a big fan of parathas – there's always an industrial-sized pack in the freezer ready to mop up any curry I make. However, their buttery, flaky texture makes them perfect for this intercontinental fusion that none of us realized we needed.

PARATHA DE NATA

MAKES: 6   **TIME: 50 MINUTES*** **DIFFICULTY: 3/3**

- 125 g/4½ oz caster sugar
- 4 **green cardamom pods,** roughly bashed
- 3 **egg yolks**
- 25 g/1 oz cornflour
- 300 ml/10 fl oz whole milk
- ½ **vanilla pod,** seeds scraped out
- 3 **frozen parathas,** defrosted

Add the sugar, 125 ml/4 fl oz of water and the cardamom pods to a saucepan and place over a low heat until the sugar dissolves. Then increase to a high heat and cook, without stirring, until the syrup reaches 115°C/240°F, which will take about 5–10 minutes. Keep checking the temperature as you don't want it to go much higher than that.

While the sugar syrup comes up to temperature, combine the egg yolks, cornflour, milk and vanilla seeds in a heatproof mixing bowl. Whisk together until fully combined.

Once the sugar syrup gets to temperature, remove it from the heat and slowly drizzle it into the milk mixture, whisking continuously, until everything is dissolved and combined. Pass through a sieve into a clean saucepan to remove the cardamom pods. Cook over a medium-high heat, stirring, until the mixture starts to thicken. This will take a few minutes but will go quickly once it starts – you want it to easily coat the back of a spoon. Decant it into a heatproof bowl and set aside to cool.

Preheat the oven to max – ideally 220°C fan/240°C/475°F/gas mark 9.

Cut each paratha into 2 rounds using a 10 cm/4 in diameter biscuit cutter (or the rim of a suitable-sized bowl). Press the 6 paratha rounds into 6 cups of a non-stick muffin tray (press one into each cup). Use a knife to clean up the edges, then evenly fill with the custard to 1 cm/½ inch below the edge.

Bake in the oven for 15–20 minutes until the tops start to develop dark spots. Remove from the oven and let them cool completely in the tray before turning them out and tucking in!

COOK'S TIP → Don't waste the paratha trimmings! Fry them off as you normally would and dip them into leftover curries for a little mid-bake snack.

GF, EF, V   *plus soaking

This is a Tamil sweet rice dish that holds a huge amount of importance throughout the culture. Pongal is ubiquitous at all auspicious events in the Tamil and Hindu calendar and, most importantly, during Thai Pongal, a festival where we give gratitude to the sun for the role it plays in the growth and harvesting of crops. Traditionally, we use jaggery instead of muscovado sugar, but I find muscovado does pretty well as an alternative. Rice is an incredibly humble ingredient – often served plain and as a quiet accompaniment but this recipe celebrates rice and allows it to be the star of the show.

PONGAL

SERVES: 6	TIME: 30 MINUTES*	DIFFICULTY: 1/3

100 g/3 ½ oz dried moong dhal
200 g/7 oz pudding rice
150 g/5½ oz dark muscovado sugar
2 tbsp ghee
handful of cashew nuts
1 tbsp golden raisins
100 ml/3½ fl oz coconut milk
6 green cardamom pods, bashed

Toast the moong dhal in a dry frying pan over a medium heat for about 3 minutes (you don't want it to brown at all, keep it moving around the pan).

Wash the rice, then soak in cold water for 5 minutes. Add the toasted dhal to the same bowl.

Drain them both, rinse again, then add them both to a saucepan with 750 ml/26 fl oz of water. Cover with a lid, bring to a simmer and cook until the rice and dhal are both tender, about 15 minutes.

In a separate pan, combine the muscovado sugar and 100 ml/3½ fl oz of water and cook over a medium heat for about 5 minutes to make a syrup.

Meanwhile, add 1 tablespoon of the ghee to a small saucepan, along with the cashews and cook over a medium heat until the cashews darken in colour, about 3 minutes, then stir in the golden raisins.

Add the sugar syrup to the cooked rice/dhal mixture along with the cashew-raisin mix (ghee and all) and mix well.

Add the coconut milk, the remaining tablespoon of ghee and the bashed cardamom pods and mix well. Cook over a low-medium heat, stirring, for about 5 minutes until the liquid has thickened. Serve and enjoy!

GF, EF   *plus cooling and chilling

Do you ever find yourself out for dinner and struggling to decide whether you'd like a dessert or a cocktail? Well, this punchy number takes care of that decision for you – it's the best of both worlds. I'll warn you now, there's a decent amount of booze in this, but if you love an espresso martini like I do, you'll be all over this.

ESPRESSO MARTINI PANNA COTTA

SERVES: 5　　　　**TIME: 30 MINUTES***　　　　**DIFFICULTY: 2/3**

5 gelatine leaves
270 ml/9½ fl oz whole milk
100 g/3½ oz caster sugar
370 ml/13 fl oz double cream
½ vanilla pod, seeds scraped out and pod reserved
50 ml/2 fl oz (1 shot) espresso coffee
100 ml/3½ fl oz coffee liqueur
50 ml/2 fl oz vodka
a few drops of olive oil, for greasing

For the raspberry coulis
200 g/7 oz frozen raspberries
30 g/1 oz caster sugar
juice of 1 lemon

Add the gelatine leaves to a bowl of cold water and leave to soak for 5–10 minutes to soften.

Meanwhile, add the milk, sugar, cream, vanilla seeds and empty pod and the espresso to a saucepan over a medium heat. When the mixture just starts to simmer, turn the heat down to low.

Stir in the coffee liqueur and vodka and keep heating. When the liquid starts to steam, squeeze out the gelatine leaves and add them to the liquid, stirring until dissolved.

Strain the liquid into a jug and put the jug in an ice-bath to help cool the liquid to room temperature – this will prevent the vanilla seeds from dropping to the bottom when you pour them into moulds.

You will need 5 x 180 ml/6 fl oz moulds for this dessert. Add a few drops of olive oil to the moulds and rub it around to grease them. This will help to release the desserts from of the moulds when you are ready to serve them.

Pour the cooled espresso martini mixture into the prepped moulds, dividing it evenly between them. Chill in the refrigerator for at least 6 hours – do this the night before for best results.

Meanwhile, make the raspberry coulis. Add the frozen raspberries and sugar to a saucepan, along with the lemon juice and 2 tablespoons of water. Cook over a high heat for about 5 minutes until the raspberries start to break down, then simmer for another 5 minutes.

Remove from the heat and set aside to cool, then push through a sieve to remove the raspberry seeds. Refrigerate until ready to serve.

If the panna cottas don't easily come out of their moulds, run a butter knife around the edge of each mould and dunk the moulds in boiling water for a couple of seconds. Turn the desserts out on to serving plates and serve with the raspberry coulis drizzled over.

EF, V *plus freezing

I've always thought piña coladas straddle the boundary between cocktail and dessert – I mean, come on, they pretty much turn up in an ice-cream sundae glass – so pushing them slightly to create this was super fun, tasty and a no-brainer. There are two main elements to this dish, a coconut no-churn ice cream and a pineapple toffee sauce that are sandwiched between some crumbled coconutty biscuits and chopped pineapple, then topped with toasted desiccated coconut. It's sweet with a crunch, and slightly boozy (of course) – a really fun dessert to finish off any dinner party.

NO-CHURN PIÑA COLADA SUNDAE

SERVES: 4   **TIME: 35 MINUTES***   **DIFFICULTY: 2/3**

- 450 ml/16 fl oz double cream
- 200 ml/7 fl oz coconut milk
- 200 ml/7 fl oz sweetened condensed milk
- 135 ml/4½ fl oz coconut liqueur
- 300 ml/10 fl oz unsweetened pineapple juice
- 3 tbsp granulated sugar
- 40 g/1½ oz desiccated coconut
- 16 Nice biscuits (or other similar coconut biscuits)
- ½ **ripe pineapple,** peeled, cored and cut into small cubes

Add 300 ml/10 fl oz of the double cream to a bowl or stand mixer and whisk until you reach stiff peaks. Add the coconut milk and condensed milk and whisk until incorporated. Finally add 60 ml/ 2¼ fl oz of the coconut liqueur and mix again.

Transfer the mixture to a shallow tub or container, cover with the lid and freeze for at least 3 hours. It's best to do this step the day before.

Add the pineapple juice and sugar to a saucepan. Cook over a high heat, stirring occasionally, until it becomes a thick and syrupy – it'll have reduced significantly. Remove from the heat, add the remaining 150 ml/5 fl oz of double cream and mix well, then add the remaining 75 ml/2½ fl oz of coconut liqueur and give it one final mix. Set aside to cool a little.

Meanwhile, add the desiccated coconut to a dry frying pan over a medium heat and keep stirring so it doesn't burn. Remove from the heat when it's a rich brown colour, about 4 minutes.

Now it's time to assemble. You'll need 4 sundae glasses for this. Crumble 2 Nice biscuits into the bottom of each sundae glass. Top with some of the ice cream, then some of the pineapple cubes and then some of the sauce. Repeat the process with another layer of each, then finally top with the toasted coconut and dig in.

GF, EF, V *plus freezing

Fennel is hugely underrated in desserts, and it gives so much life to simple ingredients like pears. I've combined it with a really delicious cardamom and ricotta ice cream that doesn't require any churning! This has all the elegance of a fine French dessert but all the confidence of a bold Sri Lankan sweet. It's a great dessert choice for a dinner party – not too much effort but truly impressive.

PEARS

FENNEL PEARS WITH CARDAMOM RICOTTA ICE CREAM

SERVES: 4 **TIME: 1½ HOURS*** **DIFFICULTY: 2/3**

125 g/4½ oz ricotta
200 ml/7 fl oz condensed milk
1 tsp ground cardamom (see Cook's Tip)
½ tsp vanilla extract
150 ml/5 fl oz double cream
4 ripe pears
1 tbsp fennel seeds
250 g/9 oz caster sugar

To make the ice cream, add the ricotta, condensed milk, ground cardamom and vanilla extract to a bowl or stand mixer and whisk until combined.

Add the double cream and whisk on a medium speed until you reach soft peaks, about 5 minutes, then transfer the mixture to a shallow container with a lid and pop it in the freezer for at least 3 hours.

Peel the pears, leaving the stems on.

Add the fennel seeds to a saucepan and place over a medium heat. Let the fennel seeds toast for 3–5 minutes, moving them around so they don't burn.

Add the sugar and 1 litre/1¾ pints of water to the saucepan and stir. Submerge the pears in the liquid and place a lid on the pan. Bring to a simmer and let this simmer away for about 1 hour until the pears are tender and can easily be poked with a skewer. Remove from the heat and leave them to sit (in the syrup) until you're ready to serve.

About 15 minutes before serving, place the ice cream in the refrigerator to defrost slightly. At this stage, remove the pears from the liquid to a plate and set aside. Heat the liquid in the pan over a high heat until reduced by at least half to get a slightly darker and thicker syrup. Place the pears back into the syrup and gently heat them through.

Place each pear on a serving plate with a spoonful of the syrup and some of the fennel seeds. Serve dollops of the ice cream alongside each pear to accompany.

COOK'S TIP → If you can't find ground cardamom, grind whole green cardamom pods in a spice grinder or clean coffee grinder, then pass through a fine sieve to remove any coarse bits.

TIPS & TRICKES

TECHNIQUE

This is a great technique to give your vegetables more shape and character. No one wants to always eat a circular disc of carrot – it's just not appealing, but this method gives you interesting shapes that look enticing and hold a bit more structure when cooked.

CUT & ROLL

1. Prep your vegetable if needed i.e. peel a carrot.

2. Place the long vegetable on your board and place the knife at an angle, a couple of centimetres from the tip. Make a cut, then roll the vegetable about 90 degrees but keep the knife at the same angle. Cut again. Repeat this process until you reach the end of the vegetable.

3. You'll be left with a variety of pieces, no two the same shape but roughly in a pyramid-like shape.

Producing a julienne is always easiest if you start with a squared-off vegetable. In this example, I've taken a carrot. All of the edges have been cut to produce a cuboid piece (don't waste the scraps, they can also be sliced thinly to create a julienne).

JULIENNE & FINE DICE/BRUNOISE

1. Once you have a stable structure/squared-off veg, cut down to make thin strips.

2. Stack the strips on top of each other OR if you have a lot, stack them along the board, overlapping each other in a line like above.

3. Gradually work your way down the stack or line slicing each one into thin pieces. You now have a julienne.

4. To create a fine dice, get a bunch of the julienned veg and turn it 90 degrees and cut it into thin little squares. The size should be similar to the width of each matchstick. This fine dice technique is also known as brunoise.

ELEVATE

TECHNIQUE

This is the technique used to create tiny little ribbons of fresh herbs that can be sprinkled over or throughout dishes.

CHIFFONADE

1. Start by picking individual leaves (this works especially well for herbs like basil and mint).

2. Stack them on top of each other and as neatly as you can so you have a pile of about 10 leaves.

3. Starting on one side, roll the stack of leaves into a tight scroll.

4. Hold the scroll together with your non-dominant hand just as you would hold anything you were about to slice.

5. Using a rocking motion with your knife, cut small slithers of the scroll about 1 mm/$^1/_{32}$ inch thick. As always, keep the fingers of your non-dominant hand in a claw position and use your knuckles as a point to glide the knife's body along to give stability and prevent you from cutting your fingers.

TECHNIQUE

Bouquet garni is a great way to add the flavour of fresh, hard herbs into a hearty, slow-cooked dish without worrying about getting tough herbs in each mouthful.

BOUQUET GARNI

1. Lay about 20 cm/8 inches of butcher's string on your board and build the garni. I often start with a bay leaf or two or a layer of leek at the bottom because they can wrap themselves around the herbs when tied. Lay sprigs of fresh thyme, rosemary, parsley and anything else you like on top.

2. Wrap the string around the bundle a couple of times, then secure with a tight knot. It's now ready to throw into stews, ragùs and more.

3. Once the dish is cooked, simply fish out the bouquet garni and discard.

The cheapskate in me cannot bear to buy filleted chicken thighs. Once you know how to do it efficiently, it's so easy and takes no time. Also, if you're making a curry or anything with a sauce, the bones can just be thrown in for flavour.

FILLETING CHICKEN THIGHS

1. Remove the skin if you'd like to (depends on the recipe). Using a piece of kitchen paper to grip the skin can help to give a bit more purchase and take it all off in one pull.

2. Turn the thigh over so the skin (or side the skin was on) is facing the board. Use your finger to feel for the bone. Using a thin knife, slice down and along the bone. Make gentle strokes to work the meat away from the bone and repeat on both sides.

3. Insert the knife under the bone and slide it along the bone to free one knuckle from the meat and repeat on the other side.

4. Feel for any cartilage that may have been left behind and remove this too.

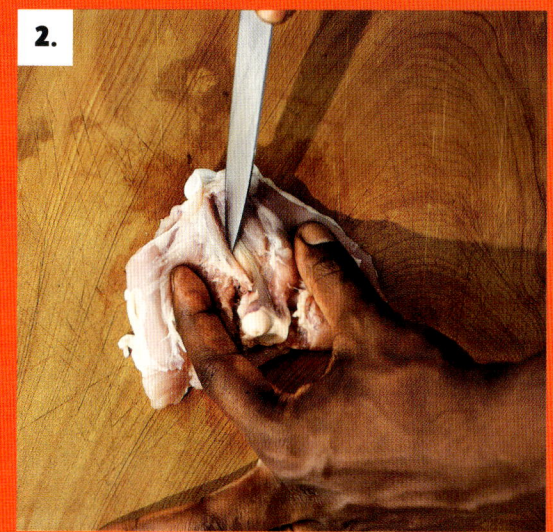

PREP

This is a lovely technique to learn to achieve even, faster cooking on round fish, plus crispier skin too. It's also a great way to impart flavour on to every part of the fish, be that through marinade or open-fire cooking on the barbecue. It's a pretty neat skill to have for a bit showing off and presentation flair, which always helps to impress.

HOW TO FILLET & BUTTERFLY A ROUND FISH

1. Place the mackerel on its side on your board with the underside facing away from you and the tail closest to your non-dominant hand. Using a sharp knife, make a cut on the midline of the belly (just above the backbone), starting at the tail and working towards the head.

2. Angle the knife very slightly towards the backbone and make long, smooth strokes to free the meat from the bones. Cut through the pin bones and work on the upper section of the belly but be mindful not to go through the skin on the top of the fish. Note: if you're just filleting the fish and not butterflying it, go through the skin at the top completely.

3. Make a long straight cut, perpendicular to the fish behind the fin that sits just behind the head. Use one smooth cut to get down to the bone. Cut straight down to remove the head.

4. Flip the fish around and repeat the first two steps on the other side, leaving you with the backbone separate from the flesh. If you're filleting the fish as opposed to butterflying, move on to step 6.

5. Using scissors, cut the back bone where it meets the head and the tail and gently work it away from the middle of the fish.

6. Remove the pin bones using fish tweezers. Be aware, pin-boning mackerel can be difficult, messy and leave you with a butchered fish! I prefer to cut either side of the pin bones and remove the strip of meat holding the bones. Be careful not to go through the skin when doing this!

7. Lay the fish, skin-side down, and use your knife to glide under the bones of the ribcage on either side and discard them.

PREP

I love cooking with mussels – taking the classic techniques but imparting my own flavour combinations to make them more vibrant and interesting. They can be slightly tedious to prepare but a few steps will ensure you prepare them properly and don't eat anything that might make you ill!

HOW TO PREPARE FRESH MUSSELS

1. Place the mussels in a bowl of salty cold water.

2. Start by discarding any mussels with broken shells. Also discard any that don't close in the water or when they are tapped sharply on the side of the bowl.

3. Using a butter knife, scrape the white barnacles off the shells.

4. Give the mussels a little clean with a stiff brush or sponge if you'd like them to be as pretty as possible (in all honesty, I don't bother with this step for a bit of home cooking!). Then remove/pull off the beards – the hairy bit that pokes out of the shell – and give them one last wash in cold water, then you're good to go.

NOTE → As they cook, mussels will open. Once cooked, if any remain closed, discard them.

1.

2.

3.

4.

TECHNIQUE

I'm a big fan of using a cartouche as there are many benefits. One of the main reasons I use a cartouche when slow-cooking meats is to ensure the liquid rolls over the meat even if parts of it are poking above the liquid-line. This means you'll never have those dry bits of meat when slow cooking. Secondly, a cartouche allows for a control of evaporation while still allowing some moisture to escape, minimizing colouration without compromising depth of flavour. Finally, a cartouche can prevent that unwelcome skin from forming on the surface.

CARTOUCHE

1. Get a square of baking paper that is bigger than the pan you're using. Fold one corner to the opposite corner to leave you with a triangle, then fold this in half to create a triangle half the size.

2. Fold the folded edge over to the other edge and repeat this step a few times until you have a thin strip of paper.

3. Hold the point in the middle of the pan and, using a pen, mark the point where the paper meets the edge of the pan.

4. Make a cut here. At this stage, depending on the level of evaporation you require, you can also make a small cut at the middle point to create a small hole.

5. Unfold the paper and you'll be left with a piece of baking paper that fits perfectly inside your pan and can rest atop the food.

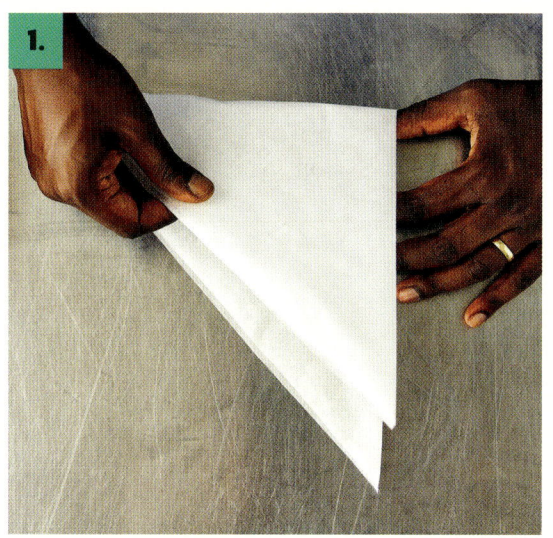
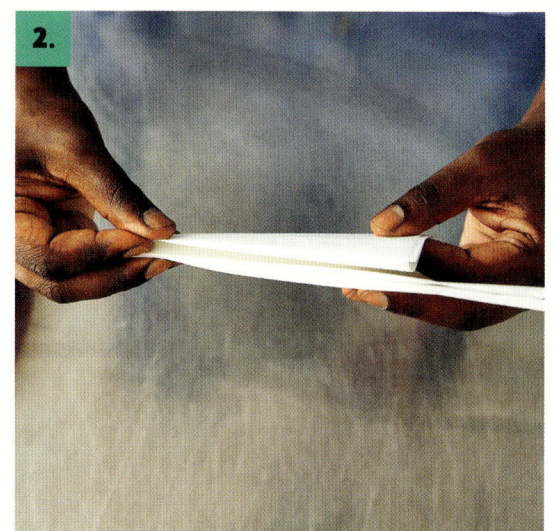

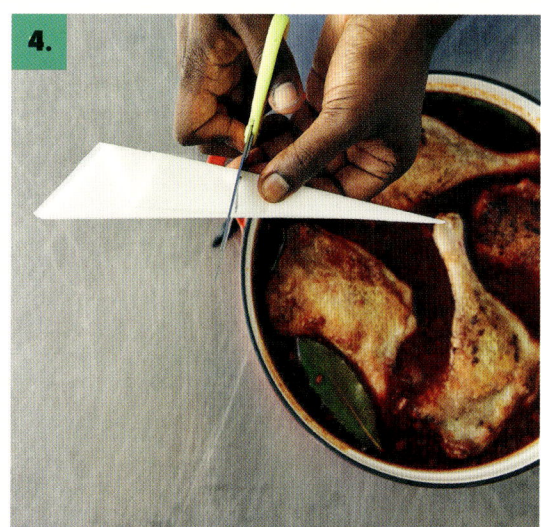

INDEX

A
almonds
  plum polenta cake 188
  wasabi chicken 121
anchovies
  arroz de tomate 161
  cavolo nero Caesar salad 40
  chicory & choy sum alla Romana 21
  Jaffna caponata 128
anise carrots & whipped ricotta 43
apple juice: sticky Marmite tofu 124
apples
  apple satay pork 76
  curry leaf slaw 16
  knuckle sarnie with spiced apple jam 46–9
  spiced apple jam 49
arroz de tomate 161
asparagus
  courgette crunch 26
  roasted rhubarb & goat's cheese salad 32
aubergines
  Amma's aubergine poriyal 104
  Jaffna caponata 128
  spiced ratatouille tarte tatin 155–6
  steamed sticky aubergine 168
avocado
  cumin beef tacos with salsa & wasakaka 134–7
  Mexican-Style Shakshouka 138
  spiced lamb & roasted chickpea salad 31

B
bacon
  celeriac & saffron risotto 141
  udon gochu carbonara 81
bananas: banoffee meringue pie 182
batata harra & garlic yogurt 57
beans
  Creamy Creole Butter Beans 146
  maleta de frijoles con chirmol 23–5
  Mexican-Style Shakshouka 138
  Sichuan beans 150
  tamarind Tenderstem on butter bean hummus 127
beansprouts: citrus cod laksa 112
beef
  bulgogi bowl & cucumber salad 77
  chocochilli ox cheek ragù 92–3
  cumin beef tacos with salsa & wasakaka 134–7
  Malaysian beef short ribs 164–5
  pommes boulangère 147–8
biscuits
  banoffee meringue pie 182
  no-churn piña colada sundae 195
black beans
  maleta de frijoles con chirmol 23–5
  Mexican-Style Shakshouka 138
black treacle: ginger & cola sticky toffee pudding 185–7
bouquet garni 206
brassic fattoush 20
Brazilian fish stew 107
bread
  brassic fattoush 20
  brioche fish rolls 177
  cavolo nero Caesar salad 40
  courgette crunch 26
  fennel & curry leaf focaccia 152
  knuckle sarnie with spiced apple jam 46–9
  kothu panzanella 116
  Mexican-Style Shakshouka 138
brioche fish rolls 177
broccoli
  citrus cod laksa 112
  Korean chicken & rice 74
  peanut butter chicken udon soup 122
  tamarind Tenderstem on butter bean hummus 127
Brussels sprouts: hot honey halloumi & sprouts 140
bulgogi bowl & cucumber salad 77
burgers: sticky tamarind chicken burgers 85–6
butter beans
  Creamy Creole Butter Beans 146
  tamarind Tenderstem on butter bean hummus 127
buttermilk
  Korean cranberry chicken wings 52
  sticky tamarind chicken burgers 85–6
butternut squash
  pommes boulangère 147–8
  spicy squasage orzo tray 78

C
cabbage
  cavolo nero Caesar salad 40
  curry leaf slaw 16
  gova varai 174
cakes: plum polenta cake 188
capers
  brioche fish rolls 177
  cavolo nero Caesar salad 40
  cured sardine royale with a tartare hollandaise 129–30
  Jaffna caponata 128
  tempura mussels with spicy tartare 170–2
cardamom
  fennel pears with cardamom ricotta ice cream 196
  paratha de nata 190
  pongal 192
carrots
  anise carrots & whipped ricotta 43
  chocochilli ox cheek ragù 92–3
  duck leg lasagne 100–3
  knuckle sarnie with spiced apple jam 46–9
  sausage pakoras with a mango & coriander chutney 55
cartouches 214–15
cashew nuts: pongal 192
cauliflower
  jerk cauliflower wedges 163
  Korean-Style Bang Bang Cauliflower 50
cavolo nero Caesar salad 40
celeriac
  celeriac & saffron risotto 141
  roasted celeriac & chickpea curry 133
celery
  chocochilli ox cheek ragù 92–3
  duck leg lasagne 100–3
  Jaffna caponata 128
cheese
  butterfly sardine Milanese with chimichurri aioli 65–6
  cavolo nero Caesar salad 40

celeriac & saffron risotto 141
charred chicory & peaches 17
courgette crunch 26
duck leg lasagne 100–3
hot honey halloumi & sprouts 140
maleta de frijoles con chirmol 23–5
Mexican-Style Shakshouka 138
roasted rhubarb & goat's cheese salad 32
sambal mac 'n' cheese 94
spicy squasage orzo tray 78
udon gochu carbonara 81
cheesecake, miso burnt Basque 180
chicken
  filleting thighs 208–9
  Korean chicken & rice 74
  Korean cranberry chicken wings 52
  peanut butter chicken udon soup 122
  pommes boulangère 147–8
  sticky tamarind chicken burgers 85–6
  Tamil chicken curry pie 88–91
  wasabi chicken 121
chickpeas
  hot honey halloumi & sprouts 140
  roasted celeriac & chickpea curry 133
  spiced lamb & roasted chickpea salad 31
chicory
  charred chicory & peaches 17
  chicory & choy sum alla Romana 21
chiffonade knife technique 204–5
chocolate
  chocochilli ox cheek ragù 92–3
  miso churros with chocolate miso dipping sauce 183–4
chorizo: Mexican-Style Shakshouka 138
choy sum: chicory & choy sum alla Romana 21
cider: knuckle sarnie with spiced apple jam 46–9
citrus cod laksa 112
coconut, desiccated
  gova varai 174
  Malaysian beef short ribs 164–5
  no-churn piña colada sundae 195
  sambal mac 'n' cheese 94
coconut milk
  apple satay pork 76
  Brazilian fish stew 107
  citrus cod laksa 112
  Jaffna mussels 110
  Malaysian beef short ribs 164–5
  no-churn piña colada sundae 195
  peanut butter chicken udon soup 122
  pongal 192
  roasted celeriac & chickpea curry 133
  Tamil chicken curry pie 88–91
  thakali kulambu 97
  wasabi chicken 121
cod: citrus cod laksa 112
coffee: espresso martini panna cotta 193
cola: ginger & cola sticky toffee pudding 185–7
condensed milk
  banoffee meringue pie 182
  fennel pears with cardamom ricotta ice cream 196
  no-churn piña colada sundae 195
cornichons
  cured sardine royale with a tartare hollandaise 129–30
  tempura mussels with spicy tartare 170–2
courgettes
  courgette crunch 26
  roasted rhubarb & goat's cheese salad 32
spiced ratatouille tarte tatin 155–6
cranberry sauce: Korean cranberry chicken wings 52
cream
  espresso martini panna cotta 193
  fennel pears with cardamom ricotta ice cream 196
  ginger & cola sticky toffee pudding 185–7
  honeymoon lentils 160
  miso burnt Basque cheesecake 180
  miso churros with chocolate miso dipping sauce 183–4
  no-churn piña colada sundae 195
  sticky Korean meatballs & miso mash 82–4
cream cheese: miso burnt Basque cheesecake 180
crème fraîche
  Creamy Creole Butter Beans 146
  plum polenta cake 188
cucumber
  air-fryer salt & pepper duck pancakes 53
  brassic fattoush 20
  bulgogi bowl & cucumber salad 77
  spiced lamb & roasted chickpea salad 31
cumin beef tacos with salsa & wasakaka 134–7
curries
  Amma's aubergine poriyal 104
  canned fish curry 118
  citrus cod laksa 112
  Jaffna mussels 110
  laksa paste 113
  roasted celeriac & chickpea curry 133
  Tamil chicken curry pie 88–91
  thakali kulambu 97
curry leaves
  Amma's aubergine poriyal 104
  Appa's barbecue mutton chops 173
  curry leaf slaw 16
  fennel & curry leaf focaccia 152
  fish cutlets 56
  gova varai 174
  Jaffna caponata 128
  Jaffna mussels 110
  kothu panzanella 116
  roasted celeriac & chickpea curry 133
  steamed sticky aubergine 168
  Tamil chicken curry pie 88–91
  thakali kulambu 97
cut & roll knife technique 200–1

D
dates: ginger & cola sticky toffee pudding 185–7
dill
  brioche fish rolls 177
  cured sardine royale with a tartare hollandaise 129–30
  sesame tuna with fennel and orange 36
doubanjiang: chocochilli ox cheek ragù 92–3
duck
  air-fryer salt & pepper duck pancakes 53
  duck leg lasagne 100–3

E
eggs
  cured sardine royale with a tartare hollandaise 129–30
  fish cutlets 56
  Korean-Style Bang Bang Cauliflower 50
  Korean cranberry chicken wings 52
  Mexican-Style Shakshouka 138
  miso burnt Basque cheesecake 180
  paratha de nata 190
  udon gochu carbonara 81
  espresso martini panna cotta 193

F

fennel
  fennel & curry leaf focaccia 152
  sesame tuna with fennel and orange 36
feta
  courgette crunch 26
  maleta de frijoles con chirmol 23–5
  Mexican-Style Shakshouka 138
  spicy squasage orzo tray 78
fish
  arroz de tomate 161
  Brazilian fish stew 107
  brioche fish rolls 177
  butterflied mackerel with hazelnut romesco 18
  butterfly sardine Milanese with chimichurri aioli 65–6
  canned fish curry 118
  cavolo nero Caesar salad 40
  chicory & choy sum alla Romana 21
  citrus cod laksa 112
  cured sardine royale with a tartare hollandaise 129–30
  filleting and butterflying round fish 210–11
  fish cutlets 56
  Jaffna caponata 128
  sesame tuna with fennel and orange 36
  tahini yogurt potato salad & harissa salmon 22
fish sauce
  apple satay pork 76
  citrus cod laksa 112
  gamja jorim (Korean braised potato) 144
  peanut butter chicken udon soup 122
  wasabi chicken 121
focaccia, fennel & curry leaf 152

G

gamja jorim (Korean braised potato) 144
gherkins
  brioche fish rolls 177
  tempura mussels with spicy tartare 170–2
ginger & cola sticky toffee pudding 185–7
goat's cheese: roasted rhubarb & goat's cheese salad 32
gochugaru
  gamja jorim (Korean braised potato) 144
  Korean-Style Bang Bang Cauliflower 50
  Korean cranberry chicken wings 52
gochujang
  bulgogi bowl & cucumber salad 77
  chocochilli ox cheek ragù 92–3
  Korean-Style Bang Bang Cauliflower 50
  Korean chicken & rice 74
  Korean cranberry chicken wings 52
  sticky Korean meatballs & miso mash 82–4
  udon gochu carbonara 81
gova varai 174
green beans: Sichuan beans 150
guanciale: udon gochu carbonara 81

H

halloumi: hot honey halloumi & sprouts 140
harissa paste: tahini yogurt potato salad & harissa salmon 22
hazelnuts: butterflied mackerel with hazelnut romesco 18
honey
  courgette crunch 26
  cumin beef tacos with salsa & wasakaka 134–7
  curry leaf slaw 16
  gamja jorim (Korean braised potato) 144
  hot honey halloumi & sprouts 140
  Korean-Style Bang Bang Cauliflower 50
  Korean chicken & rice 74
  plum polenta cake 188
  roasted rhubarb & goat's cheese salad 32
  sesame tuna with fennel and orange 36
  Sichuan beans 150
  sticky Korean meatballs & miso mash 82–4
  tahini yogurt potato salad & harissa salmon 22
honeymoon lentils 160

J

Jaffna caponata 128
Jaffna mussels 110
jerk cauliflower wedges 163
julienne & fine dice/brunoise knife technique 202–3

K

kale
  brassic fattoush 20
  spiced lamb & roasted chickpea salad 31
knife techniques
  chiffonade 204–5
  cut & roll 200–1
  filleting and butterflying fish 210–11
  filleting chicken thighs 208–9
  julienne & fine dice/brunoise 202–3
knuckle sarnie with spiced apple jam 46–9
Korean-Style Bang Bang Cauliflower 50
Korean braised potato (gamja jorim) 144
Korean chicken & rice 74
Korean cranberry chicken wings 52
kothu panzanella 116

L

laksa paste 113
lamb see also mutton
  pommes boulangère 147–8
  spiced lamb & roasted chickpea salad 31
lasagne, duck leg 100–3
lemongrass
  laksa paste 113
  Malaysian beef short ribs 164–5
  peanut butter chicken udon soup 122
  wasabi chicken 121
lemons
  anise carrots & whipped ricotta 43
  arroz de tomate 161
  batata harra & garlic yogurt 57
  brioche fish rolls 177
  butterflied mackerel with hazelnut romesco 18
  butterfly sardine Milanese with chimichurri aioli 65–6
  cavolo nero Caesar salad 40
  courgette crunch 26
  cured sardine royale with a tartare hollandaise 129–30
  espresso martini panna cotta 193
  jerk cauliflower wedges 163
  plum polenta cake 188
  roasted rhubarb & goat's cheese salad 32
  spiced lamb & roasted chickpea salad 31
  tahini yogurt potato salad & harissa salmon 22
  tamarind Tenderstem on butter bean hummus 127
  tempura mussels with spicy tartare 170–2
lentils: honeymoon lentils 160
limes
  butterflied mackerel with hazelnut romesco 18

butterfly sardine Milanese with chimichurri aioli 65–6
citrus cod laksa 112
cumin beef tacos with salsa & wasakaka 134–7
curry leaf slaw 16
honeymoon lentils 160
hot butter squid 69
hot honey halloumi & sprouts 140
Korean-Style Bang Bang Cauliflower 50
Korean cranberry chicken wings 52
maleta de frijoles con chirmol 23–5
Mexican-Style Shakshouka 138
peanut butter chicken udon soup 122
sambal mac 'n' cheese 94
sausage pakoras with a mango & coriander chutney 55
spicy squasage orzo tray 78
spicy sugar snap pea salad 39
steamed sticky aubergine 168
wasabi chicken 121

M
mackerel: butterflied mackerel with hazelnut romesco 18
Malaysian beef short ribs 164–5
maleta de frijoles con chirmol 23–5
mangetout: peanut butter chicken udon soup 122
mango
  sausage pakoras with a mango & coriander chutney 55
  spicy mango pork ribs 70
mango chutney: caramelized onion & mango chutney sausage rolls 58
Marmite: sticky Marmite tofu 124
mayonnaise
  brioche fish rolls 177
  cavolo nero Caesar salad 40
  Korean chicken & rice 74
  Korean cranberry chicken wings 52
  sticky tamarind chicken burgers 85–6
  tempura mussels with spicy tartare 170–2
Mexican-Style Shakshouka 138
milk
  duck leg lasagne 100–3
  paratha de nata 190
  sambal mac 'n' cheese 94
mint
  brassic fattoush 20
  courgette crunch 26
  roasted rhubarb & goat's cheese salad 32
  spiced lamb & roasted chickpea salad 31
  tahini yogurt potato salad & harissa salmon 22
miso paste
  miso burnt Basque cheesecake 180
  miso churros with chocolate miso dipping sauce 183–4
  sticky Korean meatballs & miso mash 82–4
  tamarind Tenderstem on butter bean hummus 127
mozzarella: charred chicory & peaches 17
muffins: cured sardine royale with a tartare hollandaise 129–30
mussels
  Jaffna mussels 110
  preparation 212–13
  tempura mussels with spicy tartare 170–2
mustard
butterfly sardine Milanese with chimichurri aioli 65–6
cavolo nero Caesar salad 40
spicy mango pork ribs 70
mutton
  Appa's barbecue mutton chops 173
  mutton rolls 63–4

N
noodles
  peanut butter chicken udon soup 122
  udon gochu carbonara 81

O
olives: Jaffna caponata 128
onions
  Amma's aubergine poriyal 104
  Appa's barbecue mutton chops 173
  apple satay pork 76
  arroz de tomate 161
  Brazilian fish stew 107
  bulgogi bowl & cucumber salad 77
  butterflied mackerel with hazelnut romesco 18
  canned fish curry 118
  caramelized onion & mango chutney sausage rolls 58
  chocochilli ox cheek ragù 92–3
  Creamy Creole Butter Beans 146
  cumin beef tacos with salsa & wasakaka 134–7
  duck leg lasagne 100–3
  fish cutlets 56
  gamja jorim (Korean braised potato) 144
  gova varai 174
  honeymoon lentils 160
  Jaffna caponata 128
  Jaffna mussels 110
  jerk cauliflower wedges 163
  knuckle sarnie with spiced apple jam 46–9
  kothu panzanella 116
  Malaysian beef short ribs 164–5
  maleta de frijoles con chirmol 23–5
  Mexican-Style Shakshouka 138
  mutton rolls 63–4
  pommes boulangère 147–8
  roasted celeriac & chickpea curry 133
  sambal mac 'n' cheese 94
  sausage pakoras with a mango & coriander chutney 55
  spiced lamb & roasted chickpea salad 31
  spiced ratatouille tarte tatin 155–6
  spicy sugar snap pea salad 39
  steamed sticky aubergine 168
  tahini yogurt potato salad & harissa salmon 22
  Tamil chicken curry pie 88–91
  tempura mussels with spicy tartare 170–2
  wasabi chicken 121
oranges
  citrus cod laksa 112
  sesame tuna with fennel and orange 36
ox cheeks: chocochilli ox cheek ragù 92–3

P
pakoras: sausage pakoras with a mango & coriander chutney 55
panna cotta, espresso martini 193
parathas
  kothu panzanella 116
  paratha de nata 190
pasta
  duck leg lasagne 100–3
  sambal mac 'n' cheese 94

spicy squasage orzo tray 78
peaches: charred chicory & peaches 17
peanut butter
  apple satay pork 76
  peanut butter chicken udon soup 122
peanuts: spicy sugar snap pea salad 39
pears
  bulgogi bowl & cucumber salad 77
  fennel pears with cardamom ricotta ice cream 196
peppers
  arroz de tomate 161
  brassic fattoush 20
  Brazilian fish stew 107
  butterflied mackerel with hazelnut romesco 18
  cumin beef tacos with salsa & wasakaka 134–7
  hot butter squid 69
  Korean chicken & rice 74
  Mexican-Style Shakshouka 138
  spiced ratatouille tarte tatin 155–6
pies
  banoffee meringue pie 182
  Tamil chicken curry pie 88–91
pilchards: canned fish curry 118
pine nuts
  Jaffna caponata 128
  roasted rhubarb & goat's cheese salad 32
  spicy squasage orzo tray 78
pineapple juice: no-churn piña colada sundae 195
pineapple: no-churn piña colada sundae 195
pistachios
  charred chicory & peaches 17
  courgette crunch 26
  roasted rhubarb & goat's cheese salad 32

pitta bread: brassic fattoush 20
plum polenta cake 188
polenta: plum polenta cake 188
pomegranate seeds
  brassic fattoush 20
  hot honey halloumi & sprouts 140
  spiced lamb & roasted chickpea salad 31
  tahini yogurt potato salad & harissa salmon 22
pommes boulangère 147–8
pongal 192
pork
  apple satay pork 76
  knuckle sarnie with spiced apple jam 46–9
  Sichuan beans 150
  spicy mango pork ribs 70
  sticky Korean meatballs & miso mash 82–4
potatoes
  batata harra & garlic yogurt 57
  fish cutlets 56
  gamja jorim (Korean braised potato) 144
  mutton rolls 63–4
  pommes boulangère 147–8
  sticky Korean meatballs & miso mash 82–4
  tahini yogurt potato salad & harissa salmon 22

R
radishes: brassic fattoush 20
raisins: pongal 192
raspberries: espresso martini panna cotta 193
ratatouille tarte tatin, spiced 155–6
rhubarb: roasted rhubarb & goat's cheese salad 32
rice
  arroz de tomate 161

celeriac & saffron risotto 141
Korean chicken & rice 74
pongal 192
ricotta
  anise carrots & whipped ricotta 43
  fennel pears with cardamom ricotta ice cream 196
rocket
  roasted rhubarb & goat's cheese salad 32
  sesame tuna with fennel and orange 36

S
saffron: celeriac & saffron risotto 141
salads
  bulgogi bowl & cucumber salad 77
  cavolo nero Caesar salad 40
  roasted rhubarb & goat's cheese salad 32
  spiced lamb & roasted chickpea salad 31
  spicy sugar snap pea salad 39
  tahini yogurt potato salad & harissa salmon 22
salmon
  brioche fish rolls 177
  tahini yogurt potato salad & harissa salmon 22
sambal mac 'n' cheese 94
sardines
  butterfly sardine Milanese with chimichurri aioli 65–6
  cured sardine royale with a tartare hollandaise 129–30
sausages
  caramelized onion & mango chutney sausage rolls 58
  sausage pakoras with a mango & coriander chutney 55

spicy squasage orzo tray 78
seafood
  hot butter squid 69
  Jaffna mussels 110
  preparation 212–13
  tempura mussels with spicy tartare 170–2
sesame seeds
  bulgogi bowl & cucumber salad 77
  gamja jorim (Korean braised potato) 144
  Korean-Style Bang Bang Cauliflower 50
  Korean chicken & rice 74
  Korean cranberry chicken wings 52
  peanut butter chicken udon soup 122
  sesame tuna with fennel and orange 36
  sticky Korean meatballs & miso mash 82–4
  sticky Marmite tofu 124
shallots
  brioche fish rolls 177
  butterfly sardine Milanese with chimichurri aioli 65–6
  celeriac & saffron risotto 141
  citrus cod laksa 112
  laksa paste 113
  tempura mussels with spicy tartare 170–2
  thakali kulambu 97
Sichuan peppercorns
  air-fryer salt & pepper duck pancakes 53
  cumin beef tacos with salsa & wasakaka 134–7
  knuckle sarnie with spiced apple jam 46–9
  Sichuan beans 150
  spiced apple jam 47–9
soups: peanut butter chicken udon soup 122
soy sauce
  apple satay pork 76

bulgogi bowl & cucumber salad 77
cumin beef tacos with salsa & wasakaka 134–7
gamja jorim (Korean braised potato) 144
jerk cauliflower wedges 163
Korean-Style Bang Bang Cauliflower 50
Korean chicken & rice 74
Korean cranberry chicken wings 52
peanut butter chicken udon soup 122
sesame tuna with fennel and orange 36
Sichuan beans 150
spicy mango pork ribs 70
steamed sticky aubergine 168
sticky Korean meatballs & miso mash 82–4
sticky Marmite tofu 124
sticky tamarind chicken burgers 85–6
tamarind Tenderstem on butter bean hummus 127
spinach: roasted celeriac & chickpea curry 133
spring onions
  air-fryer salt & pepper duck pancakes 53
  brassic fattoush 20
  bulgogi bowl & cucumber salad 77
  cumin beef tacos with salsa & wasakaka 134–7
  gamja jorim (Korean braised potato) 144
  hot butter squid 69
  Korean-Style Bang Bang Cauliflower 50
  Korean chicken & rice 74
  peanut butter chicken udon soup 122
steamed sticky aubergine 168
sticky Korean meatballs & miso mash 82–4
sticky Marmite tofu 124
squid: hot butter squid 69
sriracha
  hot honey halloumi & sprouts 140
  Korean chicken & rice 74
  sticky tamarind chicken burgers 85–6
sticky toffee pudding, ginger & cola 185–7
sugar snap peas: spicy sugar snap pea salad 39
sumac
  spiced lamb & roasted chickpea salad 31
  tahini yogurt potato salad & harissa salmon 22

T
tahini
  tahini yogurt potato salad & harissa salmon 22
  tamarind Tenderstem on butter bean hummus 127
tamarind paste
  Jaffna mussels 110
  sticky tamarind chicken burgers 85–6
  tamarind Tenderstem on butter bean hummus 127
  thakali kulambu 97
Tamil chicken curry pie 88–91
tarragon: cured sardine royale with a tartare hollandaise 129–30
tarts
  paratha de nata 190
  spiced ratatouille tarte tatin 155–6
tempura mussels with spicy tartare 170–2

Tenderstem broccoli
  citrus cod laksa 112
  Korean chicken & rice 74
  peanut butter chicken udon soup 122
  tamarind Tenderstem on butter bean hummus 127
thakali kulambu 97
tofu: sticky Marmite tofu 124
tomato purée
  batata harra & garlic yogurt 57
  Brazilian fish stew 107
  honeymoon lentils 160
  mutton rolls 63–4
  steamed sticky aubergine 168
tomatoes
  Amma's aubergine poriyal 104
  Appa's barbecue mutton chops 173
  arroz de tomate 161
  brassic fattoush 20
  butterflied mackerel with hazelnut romesco 18
  cumin beef tacos with salsa & wasakaka 134–7
  cured sardine royale with a tartare hollandaise 129–30
  duck leg lasagne 100–3
  Jaffna caponata 128
  Jaffna mussels 110
  kothu panzanella 116
  maleta de frijoles con chirmol 23–5
  Mexican-Style Shakshouka 138
  spiced lamb & roasted chickpea salad 31
  spiced ratatouille tarte tatin 155–6
  Tamil chicken curry pie 88–91
  thakali kulambu 97
tortillas
  cumin beef tacos with salsa & wasakaka 134–7
  Mexican-Style Shakshouka 138
tuna
  fish cutlets 56
  sesame tuna with fennel and orange 36

U
udon gochu carbonara 81

W
wasabi chicken 121
wine
  arroz de tomate 161
  celeriac & saffron risotto 141
  chocochilli ox cheek ragù 92–3
  duck leg lasagne 100–3
  Jaffna mussels 110
  Malaysian beef short ribs 164–5
  tempura mussels with spicy tartare 170–2

Y
yogurt
  Appa's barbecue mutton chops 173
  batata harra & garlic yogurt 57
  plum polenta cake 188
  sausage pakoras with a mango & coriander chutney 55
  tahini yogurt potato salad & harissa salmon 22
  Tamil chicken curr pie 88–91

ACKNOWLEDGEMENTS

I want to kick things off by thanking everyone who has bought this book and championed me throughout the last two years. My life has changed drastically because of the belief you've had in me and the support you've shown. For that, I will be eternally grateful. Thank you for allowing me to wake up every morning to do something I love.

To my family; Mum, Dad, Biv, Em and Ariana for showering me with love and opportunities and showing me what can be achieved with a bit of hard work, creativity and grit. Appa and Amma, no matter what life threw your way, you filled our tables, plates and bellies with delicious food throughout our childhoods and continue to do so to this day. You taught us determination and how to strive for success. Thank you for everything. Now it's time for me to fill everyone else's tables, plates and bellies with food that's nearly as delicious as yours.

To my agent, Becca and the entire team, thank you for always having my back and being on hand for advice, opinions and everything in between. Knowing that you're there by my side is invaluable.

I'm immensely lucky to have such a wonderful publisher to help bring this book to life. To Ellen, Laura, Alice and everyone at Pavillion who has put endless hours into making this book happen - thank you. You've listened to my constant thoughts (or figured out what I meant when I can't find the right words) throughout this process and made me feel heard. Ellen, thank you for believing in me from the beginning. I'm so glad we've started my literary journey together.

To the wonderful photographer, Dan Jones, who has captured the essence of my cooking perfectly in this book. It was an absolute joy to work with you to create something as vibrant and bright as I envisaged. You truly are a magician with a lens.

Holly Cowgill and Anna Shepherd, the amazing food stylists who grafted in front of hobs and 200 degree ovens in 34 degree heat and still made the food look so stunning. You're both a force of nature, I have endless admiration for the work you do.

Daisy Shayler-Webb, the prop stylist extraordinaire, you seemed to know exactly what I wanted with every shot and brought so much energy to every recipe. Thank you!

Thank you to Rosie, Sunita, Lu and El for all your help throughout the shoot and for the constant stream of iced coffees and chilled fizzy waters in the blazing heat.

Ellie and Matt, my temporary landlady and landlord over the shoot. Thank you for putting a roof over my head in exchange for a regifted bottle of wine. I loved coming home to share my post-shoot buzz with you both.

Thank you to my in-laws, Karen, Dave and the Casey clan, for your unwavering support and astute recipe feedback. Never again shall I make a fish pie with one spud.

Thank you to the friends who piled around our table to eat all the tested recipes and to those who came over, with mismatched tupperware, to take food home when I simply couldn't host any more. I feel like you should be thanking me to be honest...

Finally, and most importantly, to my Anna. From the moment this journey began, when I started my MasterChef application almost three years ago to the day, you have been my absolute solid rock. You calmed my frightened internal thoughts back then and continue to do so when stressful days get the better of me. You shared every exciting moment during the competition and continue to celebrate my wins with joy and elation no matter how big or small. You're my cheerleader, critic, leveller and best friend. Apologies for the temporary elevation in your blood cholesterol, I've calmed it on the butter now. This truly is a journey I feel like we're doing together and that's exactly how I want every journey in my life to be.

ABOUT THE AUTHOR

Since winning BBC's *MasterChef* in 2024, Brin has delved into the culinary world with full force in the form of recipe and content creation, food writing, private dining events, public supper clubs, guest judging and as a strong brand ambassador.

Rooted in his Tamil Sri Lankan heritage but with influence from around the world, Brin's approach to food is all about balance, boldness and heart. He understands how to build flavour from the ground up and teaches millions of home cooks how to do the same with his quick and easy recipe videos. His winning streak has made him hugely popular with brands and culinary institutions with whom he collaborates on recipes, cooking demonstrations and vibrantly curated content. *Elevate* is his debut cookbook.

@brin.pirathapan

Pavilion
An imprint of HarperCollins*Publishers* Ltd
1 London Bridge Street
London SE1 9GF

www.harpercollins.co.uk

HarperCollins*Publishers*
Macken House
39/40 Mayor Street Upper
Dublin 1
D01 C9W8
Ireland

10 9 8 7 6 5 4 3 2 1

First published in Great Britain by Pavilion
An imprint of HarperCollins*Publishers* 2026

Copyright © Pavilion 2026
Text © Brin Pirathapan 2026

Brin Pirathapan asserts the moral right to be identified as the author of this work. A catalogue record of this book is available from the British Library.

ISBN 9780008760632

This book contains FSC™ certified paper and other controlled sources to ensure responsible forest management.

For more information visit:
www.harpercollins.co.uk/green

Publishing Director: Laura Russell
Commissioning Editor: Ellen Simmons
Editorial Assistant: Daisy Gudmunsen
Design Manager: Alice Kennedy-Owen
Junior Designer: Lily Wilson
Layout designer: James Boast
Production Controller: Grace O'Byrne
Production Assistant: Emma Hatlen

Photographer: Dan Jones
Food Stylist: Holly Cowgill, Anna Shepherd
Prop Stylist: Daisy Shayler-Webb
Copyeditor: Anne Sheasby
Proof-reader: Vicky Orchard
Indexer: Ruth Ellis
Reproduction: Rival Colour

Printed and bound by Papercraft, Malaysia

All rights reserved. No part of this publication may be reproduced, stored in a retrieval system, or transmitted, in any form or by any means, electronic, mechanical, photocopying, recording or otherwise, without the prior written permission of the publishers.

This book is sold subject to the condition that it shall not, by way of trade or otherwise, be lent, re-sold, hired out or otherwise circulated without the publisher's prior consent in any form of binding or cover other than which it is published and without a similar condition including this condition being imposed on the subsequent purchaser.

WHEN USING KITCHEN APPLIANCES PLEASE ALWAYS FOLLOW THE MANUFACTURER'S INSTRUCTIONS